Away from Home

by Lillian Carter

LETTERS TO MY FAMILY ಈ

and Gloria Carter Spann

SIMON & SCHUSTER PAPERBACKS

NEW YORK   LONDON   TORONTO   SYDNEY

SIMON & SCHUSTER PAPERBACKS
A Division of Simon and Schuster, Inc.
1230 Avenue of the Americas
New York, NY 10020

First Simon & Schuster trade paperback edition April 2008

SIMON & SCHUSTER PAPERBACKS and colophon are registered
trademarks of Simon & Schuster, Inc.

For information about special discounts for bulk purchases,
please contact Simon & Schuster Special Sales at 1-800-456-6798
or business@simonandschuster.com.

Designed by Irving Perkins

Manufactured in the United States of America

10 9 8 7 6 5 4 3 2 1

Library of Congress Cataloging-in-Publication Data
Carter, Lillian, 1898–1983.
  Away from home : letters to my family / by Lillian Carter and Gloria
Carter Spann.
    1. Carter, Lillian, 1898–1983.   2. Peace Corps (U.S.)—India.
    3. India—Description and travel. I. Title. II. Spann, Gloria Carter,
    joint author.
DS414 .C36
954.04'092'4
                                                                77008433

ISBN-13: 978-1-4165-7660-0
ISBN-10:   1-4165-7660-6

*This book is dedicated
with love to
Mary Ida Nicholson Gordy
and to her children*

Away from Home

Introduction

MOTHER was sixty-seven years old when she made her decision to join the Peace Corps. Many of our friends and neighbors would wonder why, but the four of us—my older brother, Jimmy, my younger sister, Ruth, and Billy, the youngest of the family, and I—knew my mother too well to be surprised.

To the millions who have come to know Lillian Gordy Carter as Miss Lillian, they are just beginning to understand what a remarkable woman Mother is. Although her life in Plains, Georgia, was more than comfortable, although her oldest son was involved in his first campaign for Governor of Georgia, although she was a partner in Carter's Warehouse (which Jimmy and Billy ran) and was unencumbered by financial restrictions, Mother was never one to relax—the idea of "just sitting" appalled her.

And Plains is not all that different from other small

American communities for a woman who is widowed, whose children have all married and are living independent lives, whose grandchildren would look upon her as a babysitter and whose entertainment would eventually be watching soap operas on TV. No, Mother would never become that woman.

I knew something was going to happen before she made the announcement. I knew the signs. After all, I was with her when, two years after our father's death, she decided to leave Plains to be a housemother at the Kappa Alpha fraternity at Auburn University in Alabama, where she stayed for seven years. After she'd left Auburn, I visited her often at Blakely, Georgia, where, as a registered nurse, she supervised the opening of a convalescent home and then became its manager. But she was beginning to complain. More often than was usual for Mother, she repeated to me, "Most of the patients are younger than I."

When I went by Mother's house for coffee that spring morning of 1966, I noticed her eyes filled with excitement. "If you laugh," she warned me, "I'll never speak to you again." I knew then she had something unusual on her mind and I knew, too, she was ready for a change—but I wasn't prepared for what would come next.

"I'm going to join the Peace Corps," she said, "and, if I have a choice, I'm going to India."

Laugh? I felt so much pride I could hardly hold back the tears.

She then told me how the idea took form—not so much out of a decision to bring help to needy people, although, of course, that was a priority, but because she also recognized she was becoming bored and frustrated with her idle existence. And, one night watching television, when a public service commercial asked for Peace Corps volunteers, she suddenly snapped to attention when the announcer said, "Age is no barrier." At age sixty-seven, the invitation took on the proportions of a dare! Without hesitation, and unbeknownst to any of us, she had made preparations to resign from her job and applied to the Peace Corps, stressing the fact that her experience as a registered nurse and her directorship of a nursing home would enhance her worth in the medical field. The choice of India may have seemed bizarre to many. But to Mother, a country halfway around the globe, filled with extremes such as the Taj Mahal, the beggars of the cities, the veiled women in hand-loomed saris, the ragged sages on mountaintops, the sacred cows and unspeakable famine—these were all elements of the unknown. India was different from any place she had ever been, so India, then, was her first choice.

A few days later she talked to the rest of the family. "Gloria, I guess I'm trapped—all of you seem elated that I'm doing this fool thing! Jimmy thought it was a great idea and said he envied me; Ruth acts as if she's been waiting all her life for me to go just so she'd have an excuse to plan to visit India; Billy is relieved that I've found something to do; and you—you're already looking for a boat since you'll have my pond to fish in all the time I'm gone. Are you all so *glad* to get rid of me?"

Glad? No. We are a close family and Mother has always been our source of strength and wisdom. But we all knew she was growing unhappy with idleness and we'd learned over the years that Mother knew what was best not only for us, but for herself.

The months that followed were too filled with activity for anxiety to enter the picture. During the first physical examination, a small goiter was discovered, and Mother entered the hospital the next day to have this single barrier to physical acceptance removed.

For the first time in her life, she was required to visit a psychiatrist, and after a period of dialogue, the true reasons for her choice of medical service in India were revealed. This was one approved course she could follow to release the inhibitions she had developed during a lifetime of acceptable conformity in a racially segregated society.

Most people, if they were getting ready to leave the country for two years, would spend the last weeks at home making preparations. There were clothes to buy, a house to secure, and family and friends to bid farewell. What did Mother do? She spent her time working in the gubernatorial campaign. Walking the streets of small towns all over the state, she handed out brochures to each person she encountered, with a smile and a statement, "I'm Lillian Carter, and I hope you'll vote for my son, Jimmy."

She received a plane ticket to Chicago, and directions to report to the Shoreham Hotel where she would be indoctrinated into the Peace Corps. Except for a ten-day furlough in December, that would be the last time we would see her for a long, long time. When the time came for her to leave Plains, she packed a single suitcase, voted an absentee ballot, and walked out of her house leaving the doors unlocked, as they remained for the next two years.

At the airport in Atlanta, amidst reporters and TV cameramen, Mother said to me, "Gloria, write to me every day, so I'll stay in contact with home, and I'll write you every day, so I won't be forgotten. Save my letters, because someday, if I get home, I may want to relive this part of my life."

It was a sad time, but one filled with excitement, too, an excitement that persisted throughout the next two years as we shared her experiences through her letters. She wrote on aerograms, as no stationery was available, and they came once a week. They were precious and we shared them aloud.

"Your lives are so exciting," she wrote. Our letters to her must have been dull, indeed. Once when one of her grandchildren was sick, we wrote her about the ailment. Several weeks later, her anxious reply came. She was frantic for news about the sick child, who, within a few days, was well and back in school. We learned to keep silent about temporary distresses.

I had a letter once which made me realize that real news was to be expounded upon. She wrote, "I had four letters yesterday from different people. All of them said, 'I guess Gloria wrote you about what happened to Dan.' Then a letter from you—no mention of Dan. Dan who? A bird? A plane? A man? A dog? I have thought of every Dan I ever knew and can't figure which one! What happened to him? Did his wife shoot him? Did he drown? Wreck his car? Break his leg? Catch a fish? Get bit by a dog? For God's sake—what happened to Dan, whoever or whatever he is???" By the time I received her letter, Dan's wife had returned, and the gossip had run its course.

But even though we were careful about what we wrote, she still had her "mother's insight," and wrote me once, "I know you don't say anything that will worry me, but I can tell by your handwriting when you're upset. When everything at home is fine, you write up and down, round writing, but when you're tense, you have a beautiful slanted handwriting."

"Jimmy," she wrote, "doesn't write very often—I know he's busy. But when he does write, his letters are full of news and make up for lost time. Billy hates to write, so whenever I hear from him, it's like getting a wonderful present, but Sybil writes often, so I won't even fuss at him." My sister Ruth was beginning her career as a lay speaker. Mother wrote, "I wonder if Ruth tries the patience of Jesus as she does mine? I'll get a letter from her saying she has a wonderful exciting secret, and she'll tell me all about it in her next letter—then the next time I hear from her, she's forgotten all about the exciting event she mentioned before, but has something new to write about 'next time.'"

The second year of her stay in India, Mother's letters were filled with thoughts of food. We knew she was actually hungry, but there was no way we could get more food to her, because she could receive only one parcel monthly, duty free, and duty was very high. And, if we had, she would have given it away, or done without the few things she could buy there in order to pay duty on extra parcels. In spite of her frequent letters, we were not prepared for the changes in her personality.

Jimmy, Billy and I were waiting (and had been, for three hours) when her plane landed in Atlanta. At home, a new cabin was waiting for her, overlooking her beloved fishpond. We drove up in a new luxury car, the kind she'd always wanted. The family was gathered at her home where we'd stocked all her favorite foods, and the grandchildren had "Welcome Home Grandmama" signs along the highways, and in her yard.

We watched as the plane started unloading, and stood in awe when she appeared at the doorway—so thin, so tired, her dress much too large, and her eyes—searching, searching for a familiar face, but not recognizing any of us. Jimmy broke through the barricade first, with Billy and me behind him. When he reached her, she couldn't comprehend that we were really there.

A porter brought a wheelchair and we insisted she ride down the long airport corridors—she looked too frail to walk—this woman who had been, until a day before, walking four miles every day in the dusty streets of India. She sat, numb, staring at the people around her. As we neared the front door, suddenly she sprang up—"Wait a minute," she called—we were stunned! As she started to follow a black businessman across the floor, we reached out and held her arm. "Mother, what on earth are you doing?" "Let me go, don't you understand? He's an Indian, and he doesn't know anybody here—I've got to stop him and talk to him— he must be homesick and he'll be so glad to see me."

We looked at each other—and then we understood. Our Indian Mother had returned to America, but it would be a while yet before our Mother was really at home.

And so, these are her letters. Tales of the people she met, worked with, and learned to love as her own. Portraits of the people whose lives were changed by knowing her. Some whose fate she was never to know. But all of whom she has never forgotten. "My going to India strengthened my faith in God, and made my relationships with other people take on real meaning. If it weren't for leaving home again, I'd spend the rest of my life in India—I'm still torn between this life and my life there." It is a time she recalls as the most meaningful experience of her whole life.

GLORIA CARTER SPANN

Chicago:

IN PREPARATION

∾§ SHOREHAM HOTEL, CHICAGO

September 10, 1966

My Peace Corps career began today. Breakfast at home, lunch on the plane, and dinner with Indians, including a beautiful Hindu woman who will be my language teacher.

There certainly doesn't seem to be any hardship here. The hotel isn't as swanky as the stationery, but my room is very comfortable. Have a nice young roommate but I think she'd rather be with someone nearer her own age, so I'll try to trade her off for an older model.

September 14, 1966

This is the hardest thing I have ever encountered. I go to class all day, and I feel I'm doing poorly. Then we have family planning lectures at night. The meals are adequate, but when we have Indian food, the best I can say is B-L-A-H! I walk all the time, and don't use the elevator, so I get enough exercise to be really tired. I just can't think of anything except how Jimmy's election is going to come out today. I called the headquarters in Atlanta, and they said they didn't KNOW yet. God, what he must be going through! If he doesn't win, I don't think I can stand it— but I have to, or else I'll flunk this language course, and everybody will think I'm too old to learn!

September 17, 1966

I simply couldn't write last night. When I heard of Jimmy's defeat, I just had to get by myself and grieve over it. I decided I had to quit worrying, and just be proud that he ran such a wonderful race, and keep on going day by day trying to do my best. I must not worry about anything else.

September 21, 1966

Well, I got another roommate, nearer my age. Her name is Dorothy Bradley, and she's a pharmacist. Also have another friend our age named Mabel Yewell. The three of us pal around together, but we're no good to practice language (Marathi) with each other, because none of us is any good.

At home, they'd think of the Indians as blacks. It is so different to be here, because I don't believe there's a segregationist in the whole group.

I really feel at home in the family planning group. My medical knowledge is returning, and I'm getting used to being taught the facts of life by a young black man. Lord, folks in Plains would have a fit!

September 25, 1966

Oh, God! This Marathi is so hard! I had to cheer myself up today, so I found a beauty parlor and had my hair done. I told him to make it simple, but he piled it on top of my head. I slipped into the Pub for a martini, and the olive helped me to stand the hairdo.

I don't have a thing to read. Please, somebody, send me any kind of paperback books!

October 2, 1966

I am making so many friends now, and I'd like for you to meet some of them:

"Smiley," but he de-selected himself today, and we all felt just like he'd died!

Jim and Marian, who look exactly like Civil Rights marchers (they are). They're also atheists.

Holt, looks just like Jesus, and I think he's some kind of minister.

John, a bushy-haired Harvard man, who organizes complaints so we get better and hotter food.

Mark and Jerry, the know-it-alls. They have their hands up with questions all the time, and take over every discussion.

Lynn, whom I haven't really seen yet, her bangs are so long, but I know her by her woolen sox and scuffies.

Diane is tall, blond and brilliant!

Bruce has bushy eyebrows and perpetually sucks on a pipe.

Lennie is fat and sweet, and almost faints every time he has a shot.

These are some of the loveliest people I have ever known!

October 3, 1966

This life is NOTHING like I imagined. Early every morning, I meet this cross old man who lives in the hotel, and his little white dog. I say "Good morning," the dog says "Yap, yap," the old man says "Shuddup," and that's the way I start my day.

I've found out you have to be perfect to BE in the Peace Corps. Twice a week, a psychiatrist comes out to eat with us and let us know we're being watched, so we'll stay under a strain. I asked one of the teachers about it, and he said, "We hardly ever de-select anyone. We just make it so tough they de-select themselves."

That I damn well know!

I'M STICKING!

October 6, 1966

Whew! I had a session with the psychiatrist, and I'm still in the Peace Corps. He asked me every question in the world. Then he made me tell him my innermost thoughts, and put it all on tape. When he finished, he asked me if there was anything I wanted to ask him.

I said, "Yes, how did I do?"

He said I'd be judged on my classes, how I got along with other people and what my teachers thought of me.

What a relief!

October 11, 1966

They are having an Indian wedding downstairs tonight, but I got permission to study instead.

I didn't want to go because I'm homesick, and really wanted to cry.

I'd die if anyone saw me—so I'm sitting here in the middle of my bed, writing and eating a Hershey bar. There is just so much pressure put on us, and if I'd known it would be like this I wouldn't have volunteered—

I'm just too blue to write, but I have to. I'm thinking of my wonderful young friends here, and the older ones too— but, tonight, I need my own folks.

October 14, 1966

We were told today that from now on, we wouldn't have a spare minute except on Sunday. I don't know why anyone would waste breath saying it, because we don't have a spare minute now!

Holt, the bearded minister, and I had a discussion, and he asked me what my favorite chapter was in the Bible. I told him it was Philemon, so we read it together, and we had a little prayer. It was a wonderful time—one I'll always remember.

I saw a Chicago Sun-Times yesterday, with a double page about Wallace and Maddox. I am absolutely sick of Georgia politics—but I want to hear EVERYTHING that happens.

I'll think of something pleasant.

Oh, I'm in a "fast" class now, and learning my Marathi dialogues just like everyone else. Since the dialogues are mostly about family planning, they are sorta spicy, and we can hardly wait to get to the next one!

Actually, my work in family planning here seems to consist solely of passing out brochures from house to house. We also have interviews and lectures, but last night, I skipped the lecture and sat down in the lobby. They held the Illinois Democratic Convention here in the hotel, so I wanted to watch the Democrats. I saw Senator Douglas, Schlesinger and Adam Clayton Powell as they came in!

Well, I'm getting around to being normal again. Some people here I love—some I like—some I like and love—some I love and don't like—and some I purely do NOT like.

At first, I thought I just had to get along with everybody, always agree with everything, and never feel any animosity.

Then, one of the psychiatrists said, "Get mad—have a natural anger—cuss somebody out—throw something!"

That eased my mind, because then I felt free to just be ME!

October 29, 1966

It is time for de-selection. Some will be sent home for health reasons, some because they can't learn the Marathi, and some for being too obnoxious. It is such a strain, like being threatened all the time. I'm NOT leaving—they might SEND me—so if I have to leave, please, please don't blame me, for God's sake! I don't see HOW I can try any harder, but I will.

I think we all have battle fatigue!

I haven't ever complained, or sought any medical advice. The only thing is, there are four or five people here that probably don't like me, and I can't find ANYTHING in them to like, either.

November 4, 1966

I've been trying to study harder, but I have no more brains per hour and/or no more hours for brain.

Our lecturer tonight is from Pakistan. Since they aren't

speaking to India now, the Peace Corps in Washington vetoed our having him, but we're getting him, anyway. We're all looking forward to it, since it's something controversial.

At the present time, I feel I deserve no criticism from anyone. I am independent, surely, and I seem to be bothering no one. In fact, my well-being seems to be the concern of very few people in this world of millions.

Oh, I'll tell you what's wrong. A bunch of them got the idea I might have a little political influence (I know better) and asked me to write Bobby Kennedy and invite him to visit us for a morale booster. I just got a letter saying he wasn't planning to be in Chicago soon—so—O.K.!

I go to sleep every night thinking of home—my bed—my things—my children—my grandchildren—even my hoe and shovel.

November 9, 1966

Oh, Lordy, I've got a problem—I think.

The psychiatrist said that everything about me is positive, according to the others' evaluations of me. Then he said three people think I'm too friendly, to the point that my sincerity is doubtful. He said he thought it was because I was Southern, and that was my natural manner. Frankly, it hurt some, but he finally said, "Don't try to change your personality, Mrs. Carter, you'd be a mess!"

My roommate, Dorothy, is thinking of moving in with Mabel. Oh, Boy! If she does, I'll *nearly* have it made—just think—A LITTLE PRIVACY!

November 11, 1966

It's funny, but now everyone seems to know that I'm desperate for any kind of news about politics. I found an Atlanta Constitution at one of the newsstands, and read even the want ads three times. Everybody watches TV and they all report to me everything they hear about Georgia.

I have had an impossible task—finally found something I *could not do*. I had to fill out an evaluation of the others, and was to single out five who should not be allowed to go—but I couldn't. I just wrote in the space, "I think everyone is trying, and I believe each one has something to offer."

November 12, 1966

Well, Thank God I bumped my leg and had an excuse to stay in yesterday instead of walking all over Chicago handing out family planning brochures! They asked me if I could type, and I said *yes*. Well, after everybody else left, I locked the door and looked at the typewriter—then I looked out the window to see how far it was to the ground. (I didn't want to mess myself up too bad if I decided to jump.) I finally figured out how to put the paper in, and after fooling with it thirty minutes, mashed the right button to make a capital letter. It took me another hour to find out that long thing on the bottom made the space between words. It took me all day to address forty envelopes, and I'm afraid they'll think I did such a good job they might ask me to do this every time!

Lord, won't I ever learn to say "No"?

November 13, 1966

I used to worry about being de-selected and having to go home as a reject, but now I don't think about it anymore. (1) I don't have time, (2) I'm too tired to think about anything and (3) I've decided if it has to be anyone, it might as well be me, and that's just my hard luck! I look around at all my lovely friends here, and they're all trying just as hard as I am. Actually, I worry more about that big airport in New York than anything else. I just know I'll *never* be able to find the right plane, and I can see myself wandering around up there the rest of my life, while everybody else flies merrily off to India!

All this language I'm cramming into my brain—when we have the exam, I won't be able to answer my own name!

November 18, 1966

Well, the exams are over, and now I feel wonderful, excited, and I love everybody. I'm glad to hear that Jimmy and Vandiver are fishing in Florida. I know now that Jimmy has accepted his defeat and has had time to rest up. I'm not going to guess what he's fishing *for*!

November 22, 1966

There's been a rumor that some of us will be de-selected at the last minute, so we've decided that if that happens, we'll all quit. We have been through so much together, and are so close as a group. Really, some of these folks I'll never forget—and some I wouldn't miss if I never saw them again —but I haven't had a single cross word with anyone since I've been here. I haven't had a solitary hurt, except my feet, and I'm going to get some comfortable shoes and solve that problem.

I'm not going to say this again—but I need to get it off my chest. I'm a little scared. All this India stuff may SOUND romantic, but deep within me, I know there's another side to it. This is something I just won't let myself think about. I can think as far ahead as getting on the plane in New York, and taking off, but that world beyond is just a great big IF and WHEN . . . But, I know that when I get somewhere, I'll be O.K.

India:

LEAVE-TAKING

≈§ IN THE AIR BETWEEN LONDON
AND ROME

December 13, 1966

Well, I'll admit that my leave-taking was spectacular, but a little embarrassing, what with the TV, reporters and all. I couldn't find anybody at Kennedy Airport for two hours after I got there and then one by one the group started gathering. I was paged while I was getting checked through Air India, and the only thing I could think of was "My God, I've been de-selected!" But no! It was a photographer from Stars and Stripes, and one of the men in the group said, "Lilly, that IS fame!"

I'm not going to do a travelogue, but did enjoy London. We had time to go to Buckingham Palace for the Changing of the Guard. We were cold, so Mabel and I finally figured out the only way to get warm would be to go back to the hotel and get in a tub of hot water.

We came over with a group of PCV's from Missouri.

About ten percent of them are nice, but I don't see how the others made it.

December 15, 1966

I have my days mixed up, and can't figure out what the date or hour is at home, but I'm in New Delhi. We came from London via Rome (where we stayed on the plane) and Beirut, Lebanon. We got off the plane just to feel the intrigue in the air. It was like a movie set.

When we got to New Delhi, everything was just as I had imagined. Poverty abounding, and little hungry children begging and running around half-naked.

A reporter and photographers from Associated Press escorted me around the city to get a story and some pictures. It was a great way to have a free sightseeing tour, and they gave me a lei of marigolds. The gardens are beautiful, and I'm fascinated by the little green parrots in the trees.

December 18, 1966

I guess we're being indoctrinated. We had to attend a reception at the American Embassy. Ambassador Chester Bowles talked, and I went sound asleep. He was in a hurry, and it was dull!

We are acting like tourists. We chartered a bus to visit the Taj Mahal. We had to remove our shoes and wear cloth slippers. I tripped on mine and literally fell up the steps. The most beautiful places I saw were the burial grounds of Gandhi and Nehru.

I'm beginning to realize how different it is here. When we're in the hotel, the poverty is left outside the gates, but the waiters and porters look hungry, so, you know me—I tip so generously I'll never get my budget balanced. Oh, well, and I've found out that Mabel and I will be together. We will soon hate each other, I'm sure.

◆§ ON ARRIVAL IN BOMBAY

December 21, 1966

What a trip! We rode the train for thirteen hours, mostly through the desert. Dust came in every crack. It finally got so thick it just sifted through and went out the other side of the train. We were in a compartment with a young couple, and we all slept on bedrolls.

37

I had to get a lawyer to help me get my radio registered at the post office. He was so interested in America, I wish I had had time to talk with him, but we just stayed at his office long enough to have tea.

Godrej Colony:

MY NEW HOME

◆§ 13/6 GODREJ COLONY—VIKHROLI
BOMBAY

December 22, 1966

Mabel and I are home! This is such a wonderful experience for me, and I want to share it with all of you. Each
day is more fascinating than the last.

This is our position: we are in the Peace Corps, under
the Indian Government, and working in Family Planning
for Godrej Industries. The Godrej Colony is about thirty
miles from Bombay. There are no stores here, Godrej is an
industrial complex, with all types of factories, and they
have their own health program, cooking classes, school,
gymnasium—everything except white people. Mabel and
I are the only two here!

They will allow us to do family planning in our way—
if it suits them. That means we'll get to know the people,
communicate with them, make friends, and then advise.
We won't have contact with any other PCV's, who have
been scattered over India.

Our setup is beautiful. We have a two-bedroom flat, with living room, kitchen and bath, and we have a balcony. We walk up three flights of stairs. The furniture is beautiful, the fabrics are handwoven, and exquisite.

It's funny, but we don't have a sink in the kitchen— there is a sunken well with a tap for rinsing dishes, and to pour out water. We have an electric refrigerator and a two-burner gas stove.

We're in kind of a valley, and facing me is a small mountain range. At the foot are flats like ours, and higher up are mud and grass huts. There are about 20,000 people who live and work at Godrej Colony, and we're in the area known as "Hillside," because we're on the side of the hill!

December 23, 1966

A young boy came early this morning to bring us eggs, toast and tea for breakfast. We have no idea where to shop for food, so until someone takes us, "someone" is going to serve our meals.

We went to the school, and I was amazed to see boys aged ten to fifteen doing architectural drawings and working the electric machinery in the mechanical classes. Very small boys and girls were making Christmas decorations from scraps of anything—toothpaste boxes, candy wrappers, just everything our children throw away. Save everything for me from now on, so I can send it here.

Well, I can't speak Marathi here—they very seldom can understand anything I say. I will have to learn Hindi.

Aloo Modawalla is going to be my boss. She is supervisor of everything connected with the Settlement House and the Clinic. She is showing us around her (our) areas, and introducing us to the teachers, doctors, and others.

I think my friendliness will take me a long way, because the poorer they are, the more I like them. The Settlement House is where widows and orphans of men who have worked at Godrej are given jobs, so everyone is kept busy.

I found out the Settlement House is called "Kendra," so you'll know what I mean when I use that word from now on.

December 24, 1966

It seems quite natural that Christmas here will be celebrated on December 31, so I'm not homesick. I went to the Clinic and met the doctor there. While we were there, a little boy was brought in, having a convulsion. I stayed behind and helped until he was all right. I loved every minute!

My first family planning work today—Aloo told me to talk to a young father of four, so I spoke in English and she interpreted. He agreed to have a vasectomy if I'd let his children see me, and talk to them. I agreed and also promised him I'd stay beside him while the operation is being done.

The little children sang a song for us in Marathi, and when I told them I knew a song, "Sandobar," they sang it with me, and we all got a big kick out of that!

December 26, 1966

The children had a Christmas program at school, with a Nativity scene, and the Superintendent made a speech about "two PCV's who had come such a far distance." My first Christmas away from home, and the most exciting I have ever had. A little boy came to our flat and washed the floors with a rag. I gave him five rupees (and that was *really* my Christmas!). Aloo and her husband gave us a jelly dish and a pair of napkin rings. They are Hindu, but wanted to share our holiday with us.

We were invited to a Lions Club celebration, and rode in a bullock cart! I couldn't sit on the floor, so they gave us a table.

I sprained my ankle.

Can't sit flat on the floor.

Don't speak the language.

Am ashamed to eat canned corned beef because so many are hungry!

We finally went to the big bazaar in Bombay with Aloo. Got the necessities (iron, sheets, towels) and some groceries, but there wasn't much selection, so we will just have to eat whatever we can afford, and forget about balanced diets. There is so much poverty, I am losing my appetite anyway, and I know we live in luxury, compared even to some of the other PCV's.

Aloo wants our ideas to improve things here, and, with 20,000 people, that can mushroom.

Rice and sugar are rationed, but we have some sugar cubes. I listen for news of politics at home, but I only get Voice of America on my radio, and it doesn't mention Georgia.

Little birds fly in and out the window all day, and mess all over, but we just consider it dust, they are so much at home.

December 30, 1966

Yesterday, I watched the workmen paving a place for classes to sit. They used cowdung, mixed with water. These classes are for illiterates to learn Hindi and Marathi—I guess I'm one of "them," as I'm trying so hard to learn to communicate.

I'm learning to eat with my right hand and drink from

a bottle by holding it up and pouring it in my mouth at six inches. (So far, I'm getting half in my mouth, and half on my dress front!)

We are able to get beans, cauliflower and sweet potatoes, but meat is just out. The women at the Settlement grind wheat and make chapotes for the workmen. They squat all day, cooking.

I just found out that some of the children have smallpox. They already had vaccinations, but the serum was no good.

I'm not as vulnerable as I was at first—I must learn to take things day by day, as they come, but how I wish for things I have thrown away.

December 31, 1966

If I had one wish, I would wish for some clean rags, and if I had two wishes, I'd want some cheddar cheese! I'd rather have a chunk of cheese than diamonds.

Aloo told me that an ambassador and a maharajah visited Godrej. I don't care a thing about seeing them—I'm much more interested in the people.

I'm glad they evaluated me "too friendly" in Chicago, because I'm making friends here every day, and if my two years were over now, I couldn't possibly leave.

January 1, 1967

Happy New Year!

Everything is beautiful today. I'm looking at the gardens and all the flowers—everything blends to perfection, even the cowdung. I never thought I'd be complimenting cowdung, but I'm just interested in everything!

We had a great Christmas celebration here at Hillside yesterday, but only the staff people were included, and none of the really poor ones were here.

I'm just doing everything that comes up—even teaching the women English while trying to absorb some of their Hindi dialect.

My reading material consists of the Medical Dictionary, Hindi Self-Instructor, and once, a Times of India (in English). I haven't heard from any of the other PCV's, but I saw an American the other day. (I guess he was American—he was white, but too far away to speak to.)

I feel as Indian as any of them—I never even think of anything else.

January 3, 1967

I asked the houseboy to empty the trash, but he said, "Sweeper does that"—and now I can't even do it, because I'll lose face. I just covered it until "Sweeper" comes tomorrow.

I met Mr. Godrej. Everyone was amazed because I simply said, "How do you do?" They all bow and scrape to him. I won't ever do that.

I am still wondering WHO is Governor of Georgia, or WHAT has happened!

I'm glad you told me about the bird supper, but Mabel said to tell you please don't write anything else about food. We bought veal and pork chops, but I'm sure the veal was mule and the pork chops smelled like chitlins. I couldn't touch either of them. We have beans one day, and peas the next. I'm all for going strictly vegetarian from now on!

I have visited some of the homes, and am amazed at the brass pots and the cleanliness. All the children are so undernourished, but spotless, and the best-behaved youngsters I have ever seen.

The ladies wanted to learn some games, so I taught them "Drop the Hanky," "London Bridge Is Falling Down," and "May I?"

Every day at three, we stop for prayers—one side sings something, the others repeat it, and so on. I'll soon know it all.

Habits and customs are so interesting, and I get more accustomed to them every day. One of the drivers brought us home, and he skidded around the corners on two wheels, tooting the horn all the time. I found out he was rushing because he was in his eighth day of fasting, and could only eat as the moon was rising.

Aloo and her husband are Parsis, and have a Fire god.

Yes! I'm getting very emotionally involved. I just LOVE these people, and if you could only see how they love us.

Please ask the people at home to pray for my Indian friends—for food and knowledge—they want to learn so badly.

January 9, 1967

Mabel's bag came, and she had a few cans of food in it. I had forgotten how good applesauce was! I'd give anything for a jar of peanut butter.

I went shopping today, and looked for something to read. I found a copy of "Oliver Twist," but it was three rupees, and I couldn't afford it. I have to save my money because the welfare office at Kendra is going to have an exhibition of things they've made, and Auntie, who is in charge, told me they had made a sari for me, so I will have to buy it.

Some of the staff women have fifty saris, and are horrified that I only have four dresses.

Can you send me some gum, razor blades, lollipops, or anything cheap—our servants have nothing!

Well, I heard on VOA that Lester Maddox was named Governor of Georgia by the Legislature. That is the first news I have heard about anything I was interested in since I've been here.

Let me tell you about the designer at Kendra, the welfare station. He draws designs, flowers, birds, etc., and the women handpaint them on the saris. Please send me a book of flower pictures so I can give it to him. He has no idea what American flowers look like, and all the people here are so interested in anything about the world outside. Most of them have never been farther than Bombay, and no one seems to care anything about them, except for family planning. My heart just goes out to every one of them, and I think I'm just too soft for this job!

I have had four days of complete inertia caused by home-sickness and no mail . . . nobody loves me, I am forgotten, I hate Mabel's guts, they push me too hard here, no clothes, no food, no nothing, I wish I were dead!

I ran home to lunch, and sat down to cry when I heard footsteps on the stairs—God! The mailman! Letters from home!

I'm pepped up, everybody loves me, I don't have enough to do, Mabel is real sweet, food is even better than I expected, and life is wonderful!

I wanted to send some film home to be developed, but the postmaster doesn't know how to send a package, so I'll have to wait until he learns how.

All the people at Kendra are my friends, but to others, they are all casters—sweepers' wives, nightwatchmen's wives, etc. To me, they are all the same, and I don't let anyone tell me differently. I visit their homes, where the whole family lives in one room, with a bed folded against the wall, no other furniture, and a gas burner on the floor, where the wife sits on the floor to cook.

I've forgotten luxuries and most comforts. They don't matter anymore—I'm just that thankful for the mat on my ironing board.

January 20, 1967

I walked home today, and just got out of the way of cows and goats all along the road. A little girl ran to me and handed me a flower. When I stopped to speak to her, about twenty children gathered around to listen to me talk. They are so precious, and those who have clothes only have one dress for school. It is washed every night. The others are naked. They eat nothing except chapotes and rice, and if there is powdered milk, it is given only to the boys in the family.

January 22, 1967

Well, the reason my mail was so irregular was because they hadn't learned to read my name at the post office!

I had tea at one of the homes yesterday. It was spicy hot, and when I finished, there was something that looked like brown rat pills that they give you everywhere after eating or drinking tea.

There was a free movie at Kendra last night, and about 2,000 of us sat on the grass and watched it. I knew so many of the people there! The ladies wear earrings, some two pairs, some three pairs, and all baby girls have on earrings.

My contacts are more personal day by day at Kendra, and I love that part of my work, but I never miss an opportunity of going where I meet new people. Yesterday, I had an opportunity to work with Dr. Bhatia at the Plant Clinic, so I met about seventy men, and they all know who I am.

This is the dead of winter and it's 90°, but I need the sun to feel good, so I don't mind the heat.

I look around, and know the people back home in Plains would think all these people are Negroes, because they are black, lighter, and even lighter. Babies are afraid of us because we are too white.

Mabel and I take vitamins every day, but we've had to quit eating eggs—we couldn't tell what KIND they were—and all the milk is buffalo milk (they roam around the streets all the time) and I just can't think of drinking it!

I'll swear, Sundays are my worst days, and I've known it all the time, but I just found out why. It's the day Mabel is around all day. I'd give a nickel for a pasture to go and sit in. We get along fine, but are as far apart emotionally as Maddox and Kennedy are politically!

I never think about how it was to go to church on Sunday. People here ask me if I'm Christian and when I say "Yes," they think I'm Catholic. I don't bother to explain.

After all the talk I heard about snakes in India, I haven't seen a one. The only thing I've found to be afraid of is riding in a car. I simply close my eyes, while the driver just toots the horn and people run out of the way—all nearly being slaughtered.

Here, tea is made by mixing water, powdered milk, sugar and tea and boiling all together—try it—it's really good.

February 1, 1967

My shoes are worn out, and I can't find any at the biggest store in Bombay that will go over my instep. I can't wear chappals, which are sandals with a strap around the big toe and on up the foot, with the heel out. My feet look terrible, so my morale is low, and I'm walking four miles a day on dirt roads.

I was told that the chappal maker would measure me "soon," but I have found that in India, "soon" is a time that never seems to arrive.

I wash my own clothes, and hang them on the balcony to dry. If I sent them out, they would be washed in a stagnant pool (it hasn't rained since September) and then placed on a cowdung bank to dry. This is one task I'll just have to lose face over!

February 4, 1967

I've just gotten word that I can receive ten dollars' worth of food a month, duty free. It would be wonderful to get some potted meat, or Vienna sausage— anything with meat in it! I've only lost about twelve pounds, which isn't bad, because I walk so much, and I eat hard candy to give me energy when I wind down.

The only thing I've really suffered from is having no reading material, but I'm getting accustomed to that, and I'm too tired to read at night.

My temper is pretty smooth, and I smile all the time. Today I'm going to talk to a group about homes in America—and that reminds me—help yourself to anything in my yard or house. I'll never have any use for all that stuff again.

February 8, 1967

Aloo said today that she would get me a Hindi teacher "soon." Whatever you ask, they agree at once—and never do!

The sweeper came and we had no water, so I saw him dip the duster in the johnny and smear over the bathroom floor.

I'm smoking a Panama cigarette to calm my nerves, but instead, I feel like jumping out the window. That's out, though, because right where I'd land a cow has just you-know-what!

Water is scarce for cooking and bathing, but not for watering the flowerbeds at the offices and plants. No wonder everyone looks forward to monsoon!

February 11, 1967

I haven't seen a thimble since I've been here, and there are about fifty ladies doing fine embroidery at Kendra. They have to wear bandages on their fingers. All these ladies are illiterate and beautiful, and have small hands. Do you think you could send me several dozen small thimbles?

I'm getting very tan, and having to grease with Vaseline to keep from scaling.

Oh, how I do love my mosquito net. It is the prettiest thing I have!

One of my very good friends had a birthday today, and I gave him a razor blade, and a peanut butter sandwich. He had never tasted one before.

We had our annual "Everybody Must Be Happy" bazaar, and sold all sorts of things. We gave all the profit to Kendra for the poor—I could use it myself. I'm as broke as anybody.

I rode home today on the big truck. When anyone passes in a truck, car, or on a motorcycle, they stop and give me a ride. There is no difference between us now. We are all the same.

My Hindi teacher learned English by reading the King James Bible! He was more interested in my teaching him the correct usage of the thees and thous than in my learning Hindi!

Mrs. Godrej asked me what changes I would suggest, where I thought I would be best suited, and in what capacity. I told her I couldn't tell what improvements the factories needed, as I had never been in any in America except my own. (That should put her on!)

I did tell her I know Dr. Bhatia needs help, and I felt I could do more helping him at the Clinic, and just being friends with the ladies I already know. I would just do anything to get to work at the Clinic. When they finish the vasectomies, all the staff are served cokes, but the patient gets nothing. At least I could console them!

February 23, 1967

Well, I got mad today and exploded! Rained it all over Aloo and Mabel! It cleared the air somewhat, though I may be asked to leave. I've just let myself be pushed around too much, and I had to stop it. I'm feeling so low—getting mad always makes me sick.

February 25, 1967

I'm sitting here smoking a good old American Pall Mall. My bag finally got here, and I had to get a bearer to bring it over from Kendra. I wish you could have seen him—he absolutely wouldn't leave until I had unpacked and explained every item in it.

I was so happy to see the books I had in it, "Kim," and "The Prophet." I just held them close to me and walked around. God bless "The Prophet"—I can read it over and over, and find something new each time.

March 3, 1967

We had a day off from work, so we went to the beach and waded in the Arabian Sea. We went to a very exclusive place to celebrate, but found that alcohol and tobacco are both taboo, so we ate ice cream, and that was a real treat!

The worst news I have is—we're on our last roll of American toilet paper.

The shoes finally came, and that was all I needed. I was nearly barefoot, and the ground is 110°.

March 6, 1967

I wish you could have heard "my" children sing at the annual school function. They sang "Baa, Baa, Black Sheep" and "Little Miss Muffet"—those were the only ones I could think of to teach them. I'm assigned to teach games and songs in my sparc time, so write some down for me. (Actually, I volunteered!)

I'm so excited! We are going to Bombay for a Peace Corps conference. Just imagine—Americans, good hotel, great food, conversation! I can hardly wait!

~§ PEACE CORPS CONFERENCE, BOMBAY

March 10, 1967

I am miserable and simply bored to death with lectures. Most of the PCV's are here, but I'm homesick for Vikhroli and the children! I even miss the truck drivers!

It's pitiful and depressing to be with some of the PCV's. They have lost so much weight, and it seems nearly all are unhappy (except me and Mabel).

We got free tickets to see a dance group at the Opera House. They would have cost ten rupees each, and I'd never spend that much to do anything!

৶ 13/6 GODREJ COLONY–VIKHROLI

March 12, 1967

Well! I'm home! The minute they told us we could leave Bombay, I got a taxi and told him to rush us back to Vikhroli. It cost thirteen rupees, but was worth every cent.

I went straight to Kendra, and everybody was glad to see me, hugging me and clapping my hand, and it was truly good to be back. I stayed and ate supper with the workers, then took off my shoes and walked home barefoot.

March 15, 1967

Great news! The Peace Corps sent us a bookcase with over a hundred books—all new paperbacks—everything from Dr. Spock to comic books to evolution. I sinned. I stole six of them and hid them, so nobody would look at the words before I did. I read last night as long as I could hold my eyes open, and got up early this morning to read some more.

Now, I have to confess something. Remember my Phillips Bible that Jimmy gave me? Well, I loaned it to my Hindi teacher, and found out later that his daughter had smallpox, so now I'm giving him the Bible, because I'm afraid to bring it back in the house.

March 18, 1967

I have to pray all the time to keep from pushing Mabel out the window—thank goodness they have steel bars over them. She doesn't get excited over any extracurricular thing I want to do, so I'm just not going to pay any attention to her.

The children and I are going to put on a Puppet Show, and I'm going to make the puppets. Good God! I don't even know what a puppet looks like—but I haven't got the sense to say "I can't"—so make them I will!

I helped Dr. Bhatia today, and gave injections to three hundred and fifty children. I am so tired and REFRESHED! I *love* busy days.

I went to a God Festival with Dr. Bhatia and his wife.
I did everything they did, and was so honored to be invited.
The god was on the floor in a little temple, all garlanded
with flowers. A man in a prayer cap sat beside it. I went
up to the god, bowed, and dropped a coin into a plate, then
someone put something in my hand for me to eat. The food
was sweet with a drop of clabber (they call it curds), and I
almost lost it on my way out. On leaving, I had to salaam
to everybody present.

I worked at the Clinic Saturday afternoon while vasectomies were being done. I stayed right in the operating
room—the surgeon says, "To PAMPER the patients."
That means being kind and holding their hands, and talking to them. The surgeon is so hateful, but I just do as I'm
told. (Now, you know I'm not the docile type, but I can
mumble "Stinking S.O.B." and no one understands me.)

We finally got our ration cards, and can get wheat, rice
and sugar now to give to one of the maids. She has five
boys, and her husband was killed. She lives on twenty-seven
rupees a month.

Oh! We had a ride into Bombay and got some canned

goods. We had eaten bread and onions for two days. Don't worry about food—we have a hundred times more than our people here.

March 25, 1967

Well, I got the package, and love the dress, but they must have put the wrong size in it. It says size 16, but it's a mile too big. But tucked inside—Glory be! Cheddar cheese! I can hardly wait for dinnertime so I can have a good old cheese sandwich!

Thanks for "Death of a President." I'm not going to let ANYBODY else read it, and have it hidden in my drawer.

I'm going to really enjoy giving out the thimbles to the ladies, and teaching them how to use them.

Good grief! I got a letter today, and they want me to write about the religion here for one of the Sunday School classes back home. What on earth would I say? These forty different gods are the same as mine!

My Hindi teacher prays to his god, and mine answers!

March 28, 1967

Fifty-four of us from Kendra went on the bus to see "Doctor Zhivago" in Bombay. I wore a girdle, and nobody could take their eyes off my hose! I had to admit, they did look funny. I have gotten so brown on my face, arms and legs, and my body is sickly white, so I've started lying on the balcony in my underwear to get some sun.

God bless whoever thought of a book library for PCV's! You should see me devouring these books. I hope to God I'll never be short of reading material again—it's worse than smallpox!

The days pass like magic, and, like the Prophet, I'll be torn when I leave . . . maybe.

March 30, 1967

It's much hotter weather than we've ever had at home, but I don't sweat. I can't get enough water to drink.

Mr. Godrej is going to America. I saw him today, and asked him to call Jimmy COLLECT while he is over there. I always talk to him just as I would anybody, and he thinks I am as good as he is (I am).

Don't worry—I don't ever take the attitude that I'm po' and hired out. But—I do have a problem. I'm trying to think of some way I can get money for Christmas presents for the hill people. (Not these at Kendra, who have nothing. I'm only interested in something for the poorer ones who live in the huts on the mountainside, and who have even less than nothing!)

April fool! I have no sense of humor, because any joke here falls like a weighted stone. But I do have my own for family planning (which I hate!). I had to visit five families yesterday, all angry people living in one house. They said they won't give children milk, fruit or injections, and practically forced me out. I just smiled and bowed and said, "Nameste, you damned apes," and left.

I'm beginning to understand so many of the customs here—when you eat with your fingers, you'll find that food does taste better. I can almost understand their way of doing away with their dead—Mohammedans and Christians are the only ones who bury them; Parsis put them on a scaffold, and within three hours they are eaten by vultures, then the bones are pounded and put into a well which is used only for that purpose; the rest burn theirs and put the ashes into a sacred river.

Oh, I looked at "Death of a President" for days before I could read it—then I read and cried—read and cried— read and cried. I'm not going to let anybody else read it, because there is nobody in this country who loved Kennedy as much as I.

The time flies—but still creeps!

It's so hot, and I've found that thinking of my freezer at home makes me feel a little cooler. (I try not to think of the food.) I am losing some weight, but I do seem to eat a lot. I got a new dress from home—a size 15, but it was loose, so I took it up, and it's good to have something new to wear.

Aloo's husband has hemorrhoids, and has been in bed for three days. Men come up to me and ask, "How is Mr. Modawalla's piles?" I answer, "They hurt and are still bleeding." NOTHING is left unsaid here, and still they are so modest, except you see them squatting everywhere.

I have fallen in love with the sweetest little dirty, cross-eyed boy. Last week, at his house, I clipped his nails, and today he came to school, and had tried to BITE them off, but couldn't. He is so ragged—the children wear pink uniforms, but he has no pants, and wears a pink patched shirt. I have his name down to get his eyes straightened. Oh, he's so poor!

God knows I want to help them, and they're too proud, and I CAN'T!

All day yesterday, I just wanted to fly home and go fishing—so today I'm sitting in my room with the door shut so I can stay away from Mabel. God is letting me stand her a lot better, but I got to where I really considered pushing her down the steps, so just didn't walk down with her until the urge passed.

I'm going through all the books the Peace Corps sent, and am almost to the comic book section. I know they meant well, but some of these are so asinine, I think they must have bought hard-to-sell stock.

I hate holidays! I'm bored to death!

April 12, 1967

I finally got Mabel to cut my hair, and it looks like "Who Shot Lizzie," but it feels wonderful. I ate lunch with one of the women from Kendra, and it was spiced hot as hell, but I downed everything—sitting on a floor mat, eating with my fingers. I really like Indian food—except—Please, no curds!

This is a wonderful day for me. Mabel and I will take separate vacations! She wants to go to a quiet place, and I want some excitement!

I was a "Competition Day" judge—that's something that's forced on the residents as to who has the cleanest yards and steps. There were six judges from Bombay, and we walked around every house at Kendra and this area in the broiling sun. The natives couldn't have cared less—we really didn't see a single clean yard—but we got free lunch at the Central Office, and it was delicious!

April 15, 1967

I can't help it—I'm so homesick every night. As long as I'm busy, I'm fine, but as soon as I'm idle, I just die. If I were at home, I'd go out and buy something for my morale, but I need so many things here—I don't have a dish towel, or rags, very little paper, and no refills for my ballpoint pen. I wish I could call home, but the telephone service is so poor, they can't hear me in Bombay.

I've been through spells like this two or three times before, and have gotten over it—I just hope I get over it this time—and soon!

April 17, 1967

Gee, my outlook is 100 percent better today!

I've given away about two dozen of the thimbles, and some of them are wearing them—in their hair!

68

The Puppet Show is turning into the main attraction for the Exhibition. We have been practicing, and even I laugh and cry every time I hear it. What was a nothing has become a something!

When I got the cheese, none of my friends had ever eaten American cheese before. Now, whenever I have some, there is a commotion—I take little pieces in my pocketbook, and they beg "Lilly, please give me little cheese piece." I can't enjoy it without sharing—it's like a child watching you eat a lollipop.

April 20, 1967

The heat here has affected me very little, but it kills Mabel, and I hate to see her suffer. I don't want to be left here alone, but if she should get sick and have to leave, I would stay. I could leave anytime on account of homesickness, but I ASKED for this, and I will stick it out unless something really bad happens to make me go.

April 24, 1967

The ladies here who own a hundred saris are suspicious. They say, "We are a poor country," and in the next sentence, "How many dresses per year do you purchase?"

When I say, "Maybe three in spring, and three in fall, plus slacks and shorts," they think I'm lying. (I want to say, "Why can't you do with less and help feed these starving people?" But I CAN'T.) One asked yesterday, "Don't you Americans like jewelry—you don't have gold and diamonds like we upper-class Indians." I said, "My bracelet and Saint Christopher medal are gold, and I have diamonds and beautiful gold jewelry in America—we don't wear such things when we are doing social work among poor."

April 28, 1967

Each day, my tasks seem heavier—I am increasingly more tired, but go to bed early and kind of recoup my strength. I'm not nervous in the least, and I'm accustomed to noise—twenty people talking at once while I figure long columns, doing all sorts of book work I've never seen before; talking Marathi, even speak some Gujarati now—one thing, I have never worn off in my friendliness.

I want to remind you that I can get ten dollars' worth of food every month without paying duty, and now I feel that without it, I may really suffer . . . canned beef, Vienna sausage, beef hash, anything you wouldn't buy to serve there would be pure ambrosia.

Am barefoot now, and the road is so hot. I could use some flat shoes.

May 4, 1967

Every day, for two weeks, I have passed this woman who sleeps by the road—every day, I knew I should stop—everyone says, "No!"

Today, I emptied my wallet in her hand, regardless. I know she's starving, and nobody seems to notice her but me. I can't touch her—she's filthy—her hair is matted and filled with dirt, and I can see lice crawling—I just *have* to do something!

I've felt very deeply against family planning as I first saw it here, but now, I just almost get mad—seeing little babies as small as mice, no food, no clothes, no nothing. They say, "Nobody can make them practice family planning, it's God's work." That's a damn lie! I'm sure my God doesn't want babies hatched like fish! I reckon the madder I get, the more good I can do.

May 8, 1967

Oh, Lordy, my radio aerial broke off, and I lost the outside world! I got the messenger boy to take it to Kendra to have the aerial welded—and you should have seen the fit he had over that radio! He wanted to know if he could turn it on, and I told him he could take it home to show all his neighbors and he could play it all night. He was the happiest person I've ever seen!

I went to one of the workmen's homes yesterday for tea. I saw the wife wipe teetee off the floor, then wipe a child's nose with the same rag. When she started to pour my tea, she wiped out my cup with the *same* rag. You know what I did? I drank the tea!

Mabel is leaving on vacation, so I will be alone in the flat for three weeks. I'll enjoy her vacation as much as she will. I'm sure she wants to get away from me just as badly. I'm no fool!

May 10, 1967

That woman is still by the side of the road, still starving, drinking water from a mud puddle—and something in me dies every time I see her. When I was on my way to work this morning, I heard her holler at somebody who was trying to make her move, so maybe she's stronger than she looks.

Someone just borrowed my pen—he's either the chair back counting man or the glove cutter outer counting man. This place is a madhouse!

I worked at Dr. Bhatia's Clinic this morning, and Aloo came over in a benevolent mood and said, "Lilly, you can work at Clinic every day this week if you like." IF I LIKE???? I could have KISSED her!

May 12, 1967

When I get back to America, I'll have to learn how to go to church again, and all about WHY we support missionaries. If there's ever been one around here it's kept a dark secret!

I bought two loaves of bread today, and on my way home, that woman was dragging herself across the road to drink that muddy water. Her fingers are nearly all gone (leprosy), she's a solid sore, and was diarrheaing all over the place. I put the bread down beside her, but I couldn't look her in the eyes.

May 14, 1967

Since Aloo is on vacation, I'm free to do what I think best, so I go by the Clinic and say, "Dr. Bhatia, do you need me Sunday morning?" He says, "You can come," and I rush to get there very early. Going home, I say, "Do you need me next week?" He says, "You can come."

Very rarely he says, "You helped me get through early," and twice he has said, "Thank you."

I usually say, "I enjoyed working," and he says, "Don't mention," but he always walks me to my door.

That woman is still by the road.

May 16, 1967

I saw two cases of leprosy today. I've never been close enough to see it before. One was an old man, and the other a little eight-year-old girl. Her parents don't want her treated—they just want her to die. It's terrible—I've washed my hands until they're sore.

Ye Gods! I'm getting so involved with these people!

May 20, 1967

I've had two good baths every day, and last night my leg looked scaly, so I rubbed and rubbed, and found it was DIRT! I asked Dr. Bhatia this morning if I had mange. He said the hot wind blows sand into the skin, and the only way to get rid of it is to use a scrubbing brush—well, now I'm nearly raw!

I got a package today. I had forgotten about Mother's Day. I will take everything to the Clinic tomorrow, and wear the sandals, because everyone will have the news that "Lilly got a package from America." Dr. Bhatia says that I am breaking the Clinic by drawing crowds for injections, so they can show in-laws and children "the foreigner with white hair."

Let me tell you about the last hour. This is the damnedest country! The messenger boy (a peon) came by to get my radio to spend the night with him (he worships it), and a commotion started on the stairs. A man (Lord knows who) came bursting in and said, "You must keep these things in your apartment." I said, "For God's sake, WHAT THINGS?" A sweeper came in with a box of empty tin cans, a carton of empty catsup bottles, and eight other packages of NOTHING—he said it must be returned to Kendra. As they unloaded, another stranger came in and said he was going to get a car to transport the goods, so everybody left except one man, and he sat down and put two decks of cards together and said, "We play until they get back." Well, we play! (Some kind of rummy I'd never heard of!) After a few minutes, the messenger boy returned, the others, another stranger, and a driver bringing me a loaf of bread. To make a long story end—there I was in my living room with a peon, a driver, a labor official, and two staff members. I hate to think what the folks downstairs thought was going on—people here don't even speak to peons, drivers, or any lower caste if they can help it.

Really, I'm at a loss, wondering what is to be done in a country so hopeless that they let a woman lie by the side of the road to DIE without help—and almost killing me, because I keep on about getting her moved to a place where she can be kept decently for death. I'm afraid to say more about her. In their own way, they tell me it's none of my business—that's the way of India.

Food isn't good anymore. The woman is always on my mind. I'll be so glad when she's dead and moved—oh, dear —I wonder if they will move her!

The most enlightened person I know is Dr. Bhatia, who told me, "It's the survival of the fittest, Missy, you are banging your head on a stone wall."

Oh, everything is rosy, and I feel so good. The woman finally died, and they did move her, so I won't have to walk by her anymore.

Mabel got back today, and I was really GLAD to see her! I have been so free, and she has a stabilizing effect on me—maybe I need her.

My sweet little cross-eyed boy came to the Clinic for shots. He never cries, and was so happy when I gave him a Christmas card.

Dr. Bhatia warned me again today that I'm getting too wrapped up in the patients. He said I am the kindest person some of them have ever known, simply because I treat them all alike. He also told me that sometimes he wished I hadn't come to India, because when I leave, so many could not understand.

June 3, 1967

Woe is me! I've run out of something to read again. I'm reading Voltaire and other French short novels, but, honestly, just to exercise my eyes. They are horrible.

My nails are terrible from fooling around with so many medicines—all black, it seems. On the other hand, maybe I'm turning dark to match my friends.

Aloo has returned from her vacation, and in a burst of being glad to see me, told me I can work at the Clinic as long as Dr. Bhatia needs me. Can you imagine anyone wanting to get rid of me? Well, I've found I can make Aloo nervous by following her around asking, "What next? What next?" And when I ask Dr. Bhatia if he needs me, he nods and says, "Please come."

Sat Am. 6:30 May 27th

Wakes up @ 4 — because I went to bed before 9, I'm sure. I'm just so tired at night, thank goodness!

Really, I'm at a loss, wondering what is to be done in a country so hopeless that they let a woman lie by side of road & die without help — & almost dizzying me because I keep on about getting her moved to a place where she can be kept decently for death — I'm afraid to say more about her. In their own way, they tell me its none of my business — that's the way of India — When I say to someone, "Why can't you help us do something"? The answer "What can we do" spurts out — It's a habitual answer. The most enlightened is Dr. B— & he tells me everyday "Its survival of the fittest—Everyone wants for himself & family & noone care about the rest of world." But "Missy! you are banging your head against a stone wall" all in a mixture of "Sikun—Hindi—Marati & English". In next breath "See if you can't come over here all month of June — Another Compounder wants leave" & I say "Yes, I'll see"!

The M's & Mabel are back Monday — Its been nice having house alone — but nothing is resolved —

Aunt went to Dahr z a grocery list for me yesterday & came back z 2 cans sliced pineapple — Bacon handed the list so I could have some meat — but he said "They know nahi the Bacon" — So I have ½ small can tuna first to last until next time I can go shopping —

He promised to get me some fish Sunday AM.

But, I have vegetables (potatoes & onions) & plenty of Jello & Mangoes (Never want to hear word again when I get home)

Food isn't good any more — The woman is always on my mind — I'll be so glad when she's dead & moved — (Wonder if they will move her)

Please write I LY A 24
M

BY AIR MAIL
PAR AVION

हवाई पत्र
AEROGRAMME

65 P

FIRST · INDIA

BOMBAY

Jimmy, Gloria, Billy & all
Plains   31780
Georgia
USA

पहला मोड़
FIRST FOLD

दूसरा मोड़   SECOND FOLD

इस पत्र के अन्दर कुछ न रखिये   NO ENCLOSURES ALLOWED

भेजने वाले का नाम और पता:-   SENDER'S NAME AND ADDRESS:-

Mrs. Lillian G. Carter
Vikhroli 13/6 Godrej Colony
Bombay, 79

भारत INDIA

June 5, 1967

I have a strange feeling, and I'm packing my seabag with all my winter things, so if anything happens, it will be ready to go to America. There is so much in the papers about anti-American feelings, and some of the people here are very worried about unfavorable statements concerning PCV's. I never say anything—just smile and go ahead giving injections which are labeled: "Donated by people of America—not to be sold or exchanged."

Dr. Bhatia says, "Don't worry, Missy, no one would ever hurt you," and we continue our "integration" conversation, wondering when everyone—black, white or tan—will be able to be equal, and when he can come to Georgia and be welcomed by me and my family.

He asked me how my family felt about the unrest, and I said, "I haven't heard." Then he asked if you all wanted me to come home, and I said, "I haven't heard." When he asked me where I would go if India was fired upon, I told him, "Either to work at the Clinic, or to my flat."

June 7, 1967

It is impossible for me to keep up with the days. I am trying to figure out where all of you are, but I can't even imagine what you would be doing now.

I took a letter to the post office, and the postmaster

wanted to examine it and seal it himself. He looked at every page (he doesn't read a word of English), then sealed it carefully. He's about forty, weighs less than a hundred pounds (soaking wet), and is very snooty. I have to go in and sit while he looks through several books and papers, then he looks up and says, "Yes???" I never go to the post office unless I have an hour at his disposal. He wants a taste of American food, and if I EVER get a food parcel, I will have to open it in his presence so he can see it.

June 9, 1967

My patients are all gaining weight—they laugh when they see me and say "Hi," instead of "Nameste." They tell me their troubles in Pidgin Hindi, or whatever, and I console and sympathize in English, and they like it.

About Christmas presents for my friends here—I don't think so. I'd love to have a few toys to give, but for all the poor, it's just impossible. I'm sure there are at least a thousand children whose families I know, and they are too poor to eat, much less have a toy, so maybe I'd better just have sweets—oh, its going to be so hard on me unless they all have something!

June 12, 1967

I'm back at Kendra for a few days. Doctor Bhatia is trying out a male nurse (compliments of MY BIG MOUTH for suggesting it to Mrs. Godrej long ago!).

June 17, 1967

Happy days are here again!

The male nurse didn't work out, so I'm back at the Clinic, and even get to work on Saturdays and Sundays.

Dr. Bhatia is so modest—he says, "Missy, these people come from everywhere just to have me treat them," and tells of numerous cases that were near-death until he stepped in at the nick of time and saved them. I say, "Oh, Doctor, I don't know what they'd do without you!" He says, "Yes, yes, it would be crisis, they would decompose if I go somewhere . . . I can't have vacation . . . I can't leave them for they grieve so." He saw ninety-nine patients in three hours one day, without moving from his chair. He really is wonderful. All they need is streptomycin, B-complex, and food—they don't get food. I saw four children today who are starving. The people here LOVE their children, but food is chapotes and rice, period.

The letters from home are wonderful. The things you all do seem so marvelous, and the things I do are so commonplace.

The first shower arrived. One streak of lightning, two claps of thunder, and then rain for ten minutes. They call it a pre-monsoon shower—so—the monsoon is really coming!

I'll swear, all my prayers are answered. Mrs. Godrej asked me when I was going back to my school work, and I said, "Whenever you say," and she said, "No—from now on, your work is at Clinic with Dr. Bhatia." I have never been so happy.

When I told Dr. Bhatia about it, he gave me a long lecture: "How you help them by saying, 'Your nails cut? Your tooth clean? Where your chappals?' Now, Missy, if you intend to be useful, intellectual nurse, you say 'Come to me! I cut your nails, I doctor your eyes, I fix your uniform!' They not have anything to they house to do with." Then he fixed up a box with all kinds of medicines for itch, boils, malnutrition, even a triangular cloth to put over heads with lice, and now I am a veritable walking First-Aid Station!

June 20, 1967

Well, we have another male nurse, and I like him. His name is Raja. I've been showing him how to do everything the way Dr. Bhatia likes it done. I helped with thirty-three vasectomies this afternoon, and have seen enough operations to last me a lifetime.

My little cross-eyed boy came in today for an injection. He never utters a sound, just stands there with tears running down his cheeks. He had three boils on his face and MUMPS, besides, I could have cried! I wish he had a toy—he's never seen one. Dr. Bhatia said, "You love these patients, Missy. Don't love—you hurt. Let they love you but don't love they."

Ask the prayer group to pray for my contentment, and understanding—I'm patient enough!

I wish you could hear the storm outside. It's like nothing I've ever heard. It sounds like a big jet landing on the roof, and the wind is blowing seventy miles an hour. Everyone else is sleeping through it, but it's my first monsoon, and I'm sitting here getting used to it.

June 22, 1967

I'm feeling so damned low and useless! I have been here exactly six months now, and I needed a MORALE booster, so I went out and bought *four* cans of pineapple juice!

When I get home, I want a T-bone steak, tossed salad, a biscuit, a good drink, a haircut, a manicure, some clothes that fit, some grits, peach ice cream, a drink, some butterbeans, some flowers, and a drink, the children to spend the night, the attic fan turned on, to go fishing, some collards and cornbread, my bed, a car to ride in, my rings, a bathing suit, a good hot soaking bath to get this grime off, and some

NEW American magazines! I'm trying to imagine that all that will be available some day, and I intend to have it all . . . one thing at a time . . . as I'm sure ONE drink will knock me completely out!

June 24, 1967

What is a chapote? It's the life of India. Flat bread the size of a dessert plate, made of flour, water, salt and grease. It's rolled paper-thin and cooked on big grills until it's slightly brown. I wouldn't eat one here for anything, since I've watched them being made. I can't begin to make you understand the unsanitary ways here, you have to see these things to believe them.

I'm taking my first-aid kit to the classroom every day now, and treating the children. I just go from one room to another—speaking Marathi, Gujarati, English, and whatever, and it's working out fine. I don't think I'll ever be shy again!

I'm getting ornery! When a car passes me and doesn't stop, I call the driver names, and hope he'll wreck—then, sometimes, when they stop, I'll say, "I want to walk, thank you," and trudge on. Yesterday, I caught a ride, and when we went under the railroad tracks, the car drowned out. The driver told me to wait while he went for help. Well, I sat there in the back seat until the water was level with the seat, then I tucked my dress around my waist and waded a city block with swirling water waist deep. Was I

85

scared? Yes! All I could think of was that a snake might be swimming toward me! When I finally reached the other side, two guards were standing there, waiting to throw a rope to me to help me get out!

Have you seen a hungry hound looking at a hog killing? That's how I feel. I'm not starving hungry, I'm just protein hungry. If I had a hunk of cheese, everything would be fine.

I've learned how to cut my own hair! I roll it every night, and all I see sticking out, I just whack off.

I'm looking at the picture of Billy's family. They all look so well-fed, and the shoes look so big, flat and comfortable!

I'm smoking a Panama cigarette. It tastes like a mixture of sausage and rabbit tobacco, but at least I'm not having to look for butts.

I wish I could think up interesting things to write, but I only know the things I do. This is my life!

A delightful surprise. I went to Bombay with a group to see a movie. We went on the train, which was full of beggars. Can you imagine a year-old baby girl, just barely able to toddle, going down the aisle with her hand out, begging? You don't give them anything, if you have any sense, because you know they are begging for a grown-up.

After the movie, we shot the works! We went to a café and had a cold coke.

It was a great evening, and a wonderful morale booster!

July 4, 1967

July Fourth, and not a single firecracker nor American flag! But, glory be! What a celebration! The food parcel came, and I got word to come to the post office and open it. When I got there, all the postmen were gathered around, waiting for me. None of them had ever seen American food before. I opened it and gave them all some candy. I felt so good and independent, I gave the postmaster a can of chicken!

I can hardly wait for dinnertime, so I can eat something good, and just think—grits for breakfast! Oh, I'm so happy!

◄§ PEACE CORPS CONFERENCE, AURANGABAD
(ABOUT 100 MILES EAST OF BOMBAY)

July 12, 1967

I am at a Peace Corps meeting, but the rest of them mostly ignore Mabel and me, and I'm not interested in them, either. As a matter of fact, if I weren't going back to my beloved Clinic, I just might get sick.

I bought an umbrella for my little cross-eyed boy, and tried to get it to him secretly, but of course, it turned into a blast. About forty folks gathered around him, all talking at once, and showing him how to open it. Everybody was saying, "Mem Sahib" (thank you)—everyone but him. I have never heard him utter a sound. It might not seem like much, but that was the best eight rupees I've ever spent!

◄§ 13/6 GODREJ COLONY—VIKHROLI

July 15, 1967

Oh, goodness, it's great to be back home! Yesterday, one of the peons came to me and said, "Lilly, every day while you went, I remembered you." Now, wasn't that the sweetest thing? Not all are like that . . . some may be devils one day and angels the next—never the same.

I went to see the Hanging Gardens yesterday. They are in a very exclusive section, where the Governor lives, but, even so, there were slums, too. The Gardens overlook the Arabian Sea, and we waited until after dark to see the "Queen's Necklace." That is when the different lights are on along the coast, and moving cars look like the twinkling of diamonds and precious stones. No words can describe the utter beauty nor the awful poverty.

July 17, 1967

Oh, I'm so tired of these loose-fitting frocks. I wish somebody would send me a fitted dress! And I'll never be able to find any chappals to fit. The longer they are, the wider, and my feet just go sideways in them. I believe I have the only long, narrow feet in India!

When I went to the Peace Corps conference, I splurged and bought a little hand-carved box. It was very expensive (in rupees, that is). Remember! I live in a "rupee world"— dollars mean nothing to me. I receive four hundred rupees a month, which is equal to about thirty dollars. That is what I live on.

With that luscious box of food from home, I'm not losing any more weight. I weigh about a hundred and twenty now, and I feel good!

I'm terrified! Dr. Bhatia got a car this week, and I just know he's going to have a wreck and get hurt. He's the worst driver I've ever seen, and he's so excited! If he survives, at least I'll have a ride up the hill every day.

I have a horrible cold. It's the first sickness I've had, and I know I got it from people who walk around with pneumonia. I could use a little rest, as we saw three hundred and sixty patients today, besides the regular injections, so I haven't had a chance to sit down all day.

Raja, the male nurse, brought his bride to meet me. Her trousseau was a hundred beautiful saris. He is such a big help at the Clinic, and we are becoming good friends.

I don't care what anybody says, I can't get canned milk or sugar or anything else that goes through the black market—I just don't have any access to any luxury items like that!

Rain, rain, rain! We've been getting from five to seven inches every twenty-four hours, and honey, that ain't snow. Everything is damp, and I feel absolutely mildewed. When it lets up, I rush to get somewhere, but it catches me every time before I can get there.

But, honestly, I don't have a nerve in my body. I never

need anything other than a hard bed to lie on . . . I feel tiredness draining out of me as soon as I get somewhere to even sit comfortably.

July 25, 1967

I just found out that this is "nausea and vomiting" season. Each season has its own complaint.

I don't know how long I'll get to stay at the Clinic, but I hope it will be at least until September 1968! So much work, and so much accomplished. Never have I worked as hard, nor loved it more.

I pray all the time that I can keep working there, because it's where I am completely happy. It's where I can do something fulfilling, and God is there all the time with me. Whenever a difficult thing faces me, I just say, "God, you brought me, stay with me," and He gets me through it.

My hand is steady and my mind is clear. I just wonder where all my energy comes from.

August 1, 1967

A tall man with clipped hair and a plaited pigtail on top of his head is one of the patients. He comes in—I nod —he nods. By the time he reaches Dr. Bhatia's office, I'm there with his injection (for the Doctor to give I.V.). I put my hand on his head until Doctor finishes, then he gets up—he nods—I nod—he leaves.

I can carry on a whole conversation and never speak a word, just gesture with head and hands. You'll all think I'm nuts when I get home and say, "Aaehaa! Selah! Jao!" and nod my head, but it will be a natural thing for me by then.

August 5, 1967

I am utterly defeated! Unless I hear from you, I can't sleep or even work happily. I imagine all sorts of things— ALL BAD! You spoiled me by writing so often, and now when I don't get a single letter from you in four days, I am desolate!

This isn't a nice sweet letter—it's pure hard facts.

I had horrible nightmares last night and have to go ahead today and be as serene as possible, working every second.

When I get a letter, I can change the subject in my mind, but if I don't, the same silly things run through and through—nobody loves me, I'm forgotten, how much longer? I can't, I can't, I must, I must . . .

Oh, Hell! How I'd love to hear a silly American conversation. I'm just plain homesick!

August 8, 1967

I'm O.K. now, since your letters have started coming again.

My room looks like a florist's shop. The Head Gardener, Mr. Vinod, invited me to see his flowers, and I went by his place today. When he brought me home, he opened the trunk of his car, and in it, he had five exquisite plants and a huge bouquet of cut flowers for me. You have no idea how refreshing it is to have all this color and beauty around me.

Mabel and I had a nice dinner tonight—two potatoes and a can of roast beef. I eat plenty—just can't understand why I don't gain any weight!

August 11, 1967

Some of the backs I massage are so black, I feel like soot is coming off on me. We all get so dirty, and even washing one dress is like doing a heavy laundry load.

I get to talk about home a lot, now. The telephone operator comes by the Clinic a dozen times a day, wanting me to tell him anything at all about America. His horoscope tells him that he will visit America when he is fifty-five, and he just can't wait!

Since I'm out of reading material, Mabel and I play two-handed bridge after dinner. "It's your play, Mabel—No! from dummy—That's your trick, Mabel—No, hearts are trumps—Don't trump it, it's yours already"—and so it goes.

Mabel goes with Aloo to get the groceries now. She loves doing it, and goes wild in the store buying peanut butter, canned pineapple, fruit salad and Jello. That's all she can find, but she enjoys shopping, and I'm so glad, because I'm just too tired to go.

August 15, 1967

Happy Birthday to me!

This is Independence Day in India, so I pretended the whole elaborate holiday was in celebration of my birthday. I went to two flag hoistings, heard several speeches, and attended two teas (so that took care of dinner). The children went through a drill, and I sat with Mrs. Godrej. So many people (my patients and friends from Kendra) came up to speak to me, and I felt so at home.

A Hindu friend gave me a book, "The Art of Living," by Swami Sadhanalaya, with this inscription: "To Armna Carter who has travelled thousands of miles to our ancient land to seek fulfillment in the evening of her present life. A step towards her journey to reach the Kingdom of Heaven within herself. May our Father in Heaven make her homecoming as cheerful and easy as she is in His service through His creatures in our Country."

God! I feel like I'm on my last legs.

Well, so goes my life!

Here I am, "supposed" to be advocating family planning, and I just helped celebrate a Hindu festival, "Coconut Day." Each girl ties a flower around her brother's wrist, and he goes to the river and puts a coconut in it, and wades in the water. It gives a man virility and strength of character.

We had a constant stream of patients this morning, but Mabel and I had no bread, so I went to work on an empty stomach—and I simply ran out of gas. Poor me!

I know I need a vacation, so I'm planning to go to the same place Mabel went. I thought I'd want an exciting place, but now just want a quiet spot, to rest and read.

The Head Gardener, Mr. Vinod, sends me fresh flowers every week, and even sent some okra one day.

August 24, 1967

I dreamed about rats as big as dogs last night. I've been having horrible nightmares lately, but about things I never think of in the daytime.

My little cross-eyed boy hasn't been to the Clinic in a month. I know that he is dead, but I simply cannot bear to face the reality. It is horrid to realize that I will never know the destiny of this child; the burden of not knowing will always be with me.

I have been studying "The Art of Living." In it, there are three classes of men:

Laborers, or those who have no ideal in life but work selfishly for wage or profit, or benefit to family and self.

Workers, those who do not look for more profit but have an ideal before them, and consistently struggle to realize the ideal for benefit of society, as all great and inspired politicians.

Men of Achievement, the highest, who work neither for wages nor success. They are not after mere pleasures nor do they aspire to reform the world, but perform their duties finding peace and fulfillment in their activity.

The latter seems to be my aim at this point. Sometimes, I do not know who I am and where I'm going. These things I claim for myself.

To do as I feel I should—not to worry about what the world thinks. (At other times, I feel like saying, "To Hell with everything!")

I'm really going to study this book, not to become a scholar, but I'm just trying to exist through the most trying time of my life, and something has to give!

These are flats used by staff members at Godrej. Mother and Mabel lived in one. There are huts all over the mountain, unseen from below, but known by tiny flickering lights at night.

August 15, Independence Day at Kendra and Mother's 70th
birthday. The first year in India, nobody knew her birthday.
The second year it was widely known, and to her friends it
became a joint celebration.

A priest near New Delhi. He lives
in that opening in the wall.
Mother admired him because of
his lack of need for even necessities, and stopped to converse
with him. They didn't communicate in language, but by signs.

Mother and me. This was taken in February 1977 at the Pond House, Plains, Georgia.

Playing bridge on a holiday after-noon, typical fashion—all players sitting on a bed. Most Indian homes had no chairs or tables.

This baby had measles and a high fever. Though the child is afraid of the needle, the mother is obviously confident. (ACTION PEACE CORPS)

A favorite patient, who was brought to Clinic on a litter, suffering from tuberculosis. She came daily for an injection, and they became good friends. Note the nose ring on the Indian woman, and Mother's hairdo, as cut by the male nurse, Raja. (ACTION PEACE CORPS)

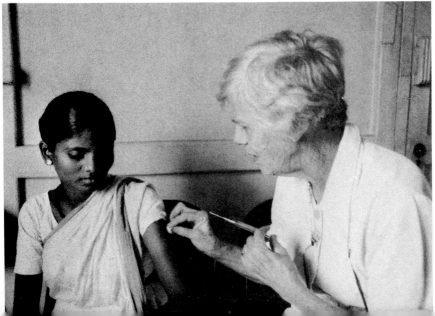

Mr. Vinod, the head gardener, took this picture of Mother and his daughter at Kendra. (ACTION PEACE CORPS)

Some of the men patients. Nearly all came for treatment, but some came just to see the "foreigner with white hair." (ACTION PEACE CORPS)

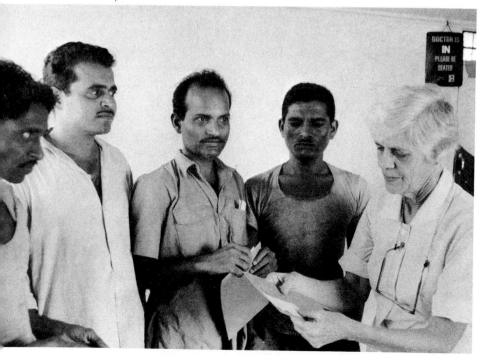

Auntie's sewing class in Kendra. These are the beautiful women who made Mother a sari with the most delicate embroidery, and for whom Mother wanted thimbles. Even young girls master the art.

This is the Mess Hall at Godrej where some staff members ate.
On a few special occasions, Mother and Mabel were invited
for a meal here.

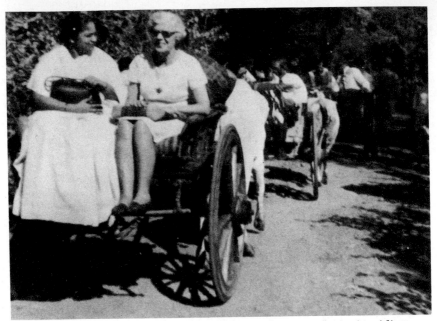

En route to a special Lions Club celebration and picnic, riding in a parade of bullock carts, the only transportation in use on that highway.

The children were so well behaved. These boys dressed up to have their picture taken. The one third from left has on typical school clothes.

After my last letter, I did the laundry to bring myself back down to earth. Then I cleaned house, and bathed and rebathed. I've gotten to where I smell! The atmosphere is salty, and all of us stay sweaty and dirty. The black actually does rub off some of my patients, but the blacker and poorer they are, the more fulfillment I have.

Gosh! Listen to me! I hope I don't go "Religious" in my old days. If I do here—it can't be Baptist—can you imagine what a mess I'd be in!

It's impossible not to think of God. Mr. Vinod invited me to the nursery today. He wanted me to see the first bloom of the "Bird of Paradise." It was absolutely magnificent—and then he cut it and handed it to me. I could have cried when he cut it, mostly because of his kindness in giving it to me.

I've been barefoot all day—anyone can go barefoot any time here, outside or inside.

It rains constantly, and where I once looked at cracked, parched earth, there is beautiful green grass. The trees are green after looking dead for months.

The one thing I HATE is doing nothing, so whenever I'm idle, I go to school to see the children. The greatest privilege they know is to be permitted to carry my first-aid kit. They are all so glad when they see me, and just turn into happy little wiggletails when I walk in.

I have nothing to read again. I go through a book like a hungry man eating a grape!

September 3, 1967

One of the drivers came to see me today, and brought his wife so she could see the "American house." He had to slip in so no one would see him, as he is a lower caste, and isn't supposed to come except as a servant. We would not have bread, except for the fact that he buys it for us on his journeys carrying staff members here and there.

Mabel got a food parcel, so we had a good dinner. Maybe I'll sleep better tonight. I've been having insomnia, and just lie awake trying not to think until two or three o'clock in the morning. Dr. Bhatia said he'd give me a mild hypnotic when I want one, but I *fear* medication! I'll just spend all my money on food—to Hell with it, I'm not going hungry!

September 5, 1967

Well, I tried to mail a package today, and the post office refused it. I had it wrapped O.K., and couldn't understand why they wouldn't accept it, so I asked Dr. Bhatia to go back with me and talk to the postmaster. When we got there, we were informed that the parcel department was closed! He acted so ugly and adamant. Believe me, I won't ever try to mail another one! I keep the post office in funds, because I have to pay heavy duty on everything I receive— I don't mind that, but I do mind being treated as dirt!

I'll be damned glad when I get back home!

September 7, 1967

I'm real keyed up—lose my temper easily—and I think I need a rest. I'm making arrangements to go to Matheran on vacation next month.

I'm trying a different brand of cigarettes. These taste like straw mixed with cowdung, and cost ten rupees a carton. I don't smoke very much anyway, but just like to have some on hand in case I want one.

I think I may try to get someone else to try to mail a package for me, to see if it's just me the postmaster hates. I know I got too upset over that incident, but if he should read this letter, I hope he drops dead!

September 9, 1967

Glory! Glory! Glory!

The food parcel came today, and everything is beautiful, wonderful, lovely, and I'm ecstatic!

I don't need a single thing in this world, and I'm just—well—I'm O.K.!

September 11, 1967

I've spanned two civilizations.

I straightened out all the newspapers that were used for packing in the food parcel, and read every word. Even though they were months old, it was like being at home.

Then, I went to a Gunputi Celebration. Took off my shoes at the door and bowed to everyone, then to the Gunputi idol, which was sitting on the floor surrounded by flowers, incense, fruit and candles. A girl put a dot on my forehead, and one between my eyes (one red, one yellow). In a couple of days, all Gunputis will be taken and put in the Arabian Sea, where they will sink and melt, since they're made of clay. It's a big ceremony, and I'm planning to go.

Aloo has asked me to wear my sari, but I haven't decided, yet. The only thing "American" about me now is the clothes I wear. I know that even that difference will vanish soon.

Last night, I had a wonderful dream. It was a year from today, and I was home.

I have to go to Bombay this weekend for a "thing" about family planning. (A Demographic something—Hell! They ain't got no sense!)

I'm eating three oranges a day for vitamins now, and spend a lot of time just looking at all our food sitting there on the shelf. I don't really care if I gain a little weight. Frankly, I'm beginning to look haggard.

Aloo wanted me to leave the Clinic and go back to work at Kendra, but Dr. Bhatia said he was going to start giving his workers leave, one at a time, so I will always be necessary to fill a vacancy.

The meeting in Bombay was great—for one reason! Lady Rama Ran was one of the speakers. She told them that instead of having the legal age for girls to marry at seventeen, to cut out the practice of marrying them off (we all know some are married while they're still babies), to educate the women, provide jobs for them, let them learn something of the world. Then she turned to the man representing the Government and said, "But, I'll fight any legislation for FORCE, Mister, and you can put that in your pipe, take it to Delhi, and tell them!" Boy, I loved that.

I talked to her, and asked her if she'd ever heard the word "Guts." She said, "Hell, yes! I learned it years ago in America."

She's the first modern speaker I've heard since I've been here.

September 20, 1967

The Hindu friend (the one who gave me the book) is Dr. Bhatia's cousin. I call him Mr. Bhatia, and I am going to meet his wife, because I am going to be invited to stay overnight in their home in November, during Devali holidays. He is helping me learn to put my many words of Hindi into meaningful sentences.

It is nice to have good friends here. I had dinner with one of the engineers and his family. His mother agreed to eat at the table with us only because she liked me. It wasn't until later that I learned she had never consented to eat with a FOREIGNER before!

I asked him why the newspapers had so much about wanting PCV's to go home, and he said it's because they think PCV's are like missionaries. He said missionaries came to some villages to help the people, and tried to turn Hindus into Christians. Then he said, "No one wants you to go home."

I have simply become color-blind. I've become as dark as most of my friends, and even the little black babies are no longer afraid of me. Tiny children run up to me and hold out their little hands for me to kiss.

One of the teachers brought me a pair of her chappals, because my shoes were so worn, and I was going barefoot. They actually fit my feet, and she told me she would have some new ones made for me.

When Indians love you, they do so completely, and when they hate, it is with the same intensity. My friend the peon knew that I loved to read, so he brought me a Bible in Hindu SCRIPT. (Oh, boy!)

Actually, I find that books are better the third and fourth time, so I'm reading "Anna Karenina" again.

The package of Christmas gifts arrived, and before I could get to the post office, word had spread that I had a parcel from America. I sent one of the messengers for it, so I wouldn't have to open it in front of the postmaster.

I was so excited—the stuff is so beautiful, and so luxurious—perfume and knives! I have to confess—I opened a bottle of perfume, and I smelled so good, I put on the blue dress Billy's family sent me for Mother's Day. I feel so glamorous, if I weren't so darn skinny. Now, people say, "You are losing too much weight." It's like meeting someone who says, "You look like you feel terrible."

Yesterday, a funny thing happened—I got separate letters from each of Ruth's children. They were all sweet, and I could just hear Ruth saying, "No, not one step until you all write Grandmother!"

October 1, 1967

Today is Jimmy's birthday, and I'm homesick for all of you. Please let me know the minute Rosalynn has the baby. I am so excited, and I do hope it will be a girl.

I don't know what I wish for Billy and Sybil, a boy would be nice, but all their daughters are so precious.

It's funny, here I am a million miles from home, in family planning, and the brightest thing in my life is knowing that I have two grandbabies on the way. I wish I could be there—if I ever get back, I will NEVER leave home again!

October 5, 1967

I am getting ready to go on my vacation to Matheran. Mr. Bhatia (my Hindu friend) told me that he and his wife will visit me there. I haven't met her yet, but wives are usually boring. They don't know a thing, and have to treat their husbands like gods!

Oh, I want all the things you sent for Christmas gifts. I won't have a single luxurious article if I give them all away. The bath powder isn't a luxury—it's a necessity. I use it all the time—my skin smells—even after a bath— like an Indian—they have a smell all their own—kinda . . . musky—just different—and I smell like that, too.

Mabel and I are hitting it off pretty good, for some reason. Probably because we work at different places, and see each other only at meals. One thing I yearn for on my vacation—PRIVACY! I doubt that I'll have that, because wherever I go, a crowd gathers.

By the way, there's no way for any of you to send me money. The Peace Corps doesn't allow it. I had to get my shots yesterday, found out one of the PCV's has infectious hepatitis. I don't know who, or where. Just smashed two mosquitoes at once on my shoulder. I sleep under the net every night now. Just think, only eleven more months— one more hot season, one more monsoon.

⮬ LORD'S CENTRAL HOTEL, MATHERAN

October 9, 1967

Aloo took me to catch the big train in Bombay, and we stopped somewhere and changed to a little train with an electric engine.

I was the only American among all the Indians, and I pretended I was in an Alfred Hitchcock movie, going toward an intriguing destination as the little train went up and up, around and around the mountain for hours, with its eery whistle shrilling around every curve.

A storm is raging outside this old, rambling hotel, and down the mountainside below my window, I can see lightning flashing. It is simply breathtaking.

Since I am the only "rich American" here, I have been getting deluxe service, and I'm just going to relax and enjoy it. The meals are lavish, even meat and butter, but I can't eat much—I fill up so quickly.

October 12, 1967

I do nothing except rest in my room and walk in the garden. It is thrilling to be idle and bored for a change.

I have two buckets of hot water every morning. I sit on a stool in a sink which has a drain, and use one bucket to soap myself, then pour the other over me to rinse—it's the best and cleanest bath I've ever had.

I met a prophet yesterday—he looked at me, and said, right out of the blue, "You will write a book before 1969," then he gave me his walking stick. What a weird country! As I sit here, a boy is looking over my shoulder. Of course, he can't read a word, but hopes I'll tip him so he will leave.

Monkeys on the roof are making such a racket. They sound like a football team in the attic!

October 15, 1967

I asked for a Hindi tutor so I'd have something to do, and he came today, said, "Good afternoon, Miss Illic Car," heard my radio—and that was the end of my lesson. He just sat and listened to it, completely engrossed, until I finally told him to take it with him, and invited him to come back for dinner. He returned at eight, with the radio going full blast, of course, and I persuaded him to turn it off during dinner by promising him he could take it home to spend the night.

I've never seen anyone eat so much, and the dinner was delicious—until he gave the first big BURP. You probably heard it in Plains! Thereafter, every five or six bites, another and another. It is etiquette for middle- and low-class Indians, but this is one aspect of their culture I will NOT adopt!

This is the laziest I have ever been in my life, and I'm actually enjoying it. I didn't realize how completely exhausted I had become—it frightens me.

October 22, 1967

I have had an exciting adventure. A Swami arrived with his entourage, and I joined right in, to hear his lectures, to walk and meditate. He is glorious, with his shaved head, earrings, and flowing yellow robe. He speaks about the moon and sun, and is quite inspiring. The others go through quite a ceremony when we see him, stooping almost to the floor, putting both hands on his feet, and backing away salaaming. I just said, "Bye now, see you tonight," and he said, "Bye, O.K.!"

October 25, 1967

I am sick of nothing but Indians, and no blond hair, and big butts, and having an inferiority complex because their noses are turned up always. And I'm tired of resting!

I'm so very homesick. I have to say, "Get thee behind me, Satan," because I'm thinking that maybe the war in Egypt will cause me to be evacuated, or maybe somebody will drop a bomb, and I could go home—then I am afraid.

But, when I think that . . . you know what I'm going to do? I'm going out right now and buy a paper, because if war IS coming, I'll *have* to come home!

October 29, 1967

I had tea with a Hindu couple yesterday. He and I sat on pots (stools) and watched while she made tea. She squatted on the floor, where she had a towel which she picked up with her toes (she had ten), then she pitched it in the air and caught it to wipe cups and saucers, floor, and vessel. I watched with awe, getting more unhungry by the minute. The table was about six inches high, made of cowdung, and the floors were paved with same.

When she fixed our tea, she didn't have any for herself, and I refused to eat without her—so, for the FIRST TIME, she ate with her husband. When I left, they promised me that from now on they would eat together, UNLESS someone else was there!

The wind is blowing like it does in March back home. It's the Devali letting the Hindus know he will be arriving shortly.

October 30, 1967

The great news came today—I'm so happy that Jimmy and Rosalynn have a baby girl, and I love the name Amy Lynn!

I got the clippings you sent, and Jimmy sent me pictures of her. Oh, how I'd love to see her. I could tell by his letter that his heart was just full of love for that baby, and just think of what she'll mean to them!

I am rested and at peace within myself. I have been sitting here thinking of my life back in America, and it seems so strange to me. The things that come to my mind—color TV, Little Orphan Annie, the World Series (God! It's over, and I don't even know who played!), fishing, a martini, church, my neighbors—all this seems part of another life, another world. Somehow, Hinduism is seeping into my dormant mind, and I know that, somehow, THIS IS MY REINCARNATION!

⤙ 13/6 GODREJ COLONY—VIKHROLI HOME AGAIN!

November 4, 1967

My last day at Matheran, I walked through the streets, passing out candy to the little children, who followed me everywhere.

Mr. Bhatia and his wife came for me, and I stayed at their home in Bombay for the Devali Celebration. It was a very high honor for me to be invited to participate. After dinner, we went to the temple for prayer, then I watched the fireworks while everyone else watched me!

The next day, we went to the eight-hundred-year-old temple to give flowers to the god, then were allowed to enter the presence of the Swami, who gave me a sip of water from the Ganges River.

Later, we visited a Sikh home. The men never cut their hair or beards, but wear it braided, and the boys wear lots of bangles.

All the people would come up to me and touch me—it unnerved me at first, but I learned to grin and bear it.

Everybody has been yelling at me, "Miss you all day, we remember you!" I'm so happy to be home, and Dr. Bhatia is expecting me at the Clinic in the morning!

A package arrived from Jimmy—BOOKS! I swear, I'm going to ration them, and when I get to the crossword puzzle book, I'm going to finish each one, without looking up an answer, before I let myself start on another.

Mabel has a bad cough, and I worry about her. Dr. Bhatia asked me what I would do if Mabel had to go home, and I told him I'd have to leave, too. He said, "No, you stay, Missy. We look after you."

I have been helping the public health nurse at Creekside, which is two miles from here. I don't mind the walking, but the monsoon is gone, and it's so terribly hot.

We have to go to Bombay for another Peace Corps meeting on whether or not to continue the family planning program. Frankly, I couldn't care less, and know we will just hear the same old B.S., but maybe they will serve dinner.

November 12, 1967

I went to an interesting place today, the Hindu Camp,
and heard Mr. Bhatia's Swami lecture for three hours.
He talked about separating the physical from the spiritual,
which possibly enabled me to sit on the ground listening
for three hours without moving a muscle!

When I got home, instead of floating around on cloud
nine, I listened to Mabel's constant coughing until my
nerves shot all to pieces! I picked up a glass dish and
slammed it down and broke it. Instant relaxation!

There are five thousand workers in the plants, and Raja
(the male nurse) and I are going to start making rounds
checking everyone's eyes. Bless Dr. Bhatia's heart, he never
runs out of things for me to do, he knows I don't want to
go back to Kendra and leave our beloved Clinic.

November 16, 1967

No matter how weary I am, and no matter how blue, I
try to write all of you regularly to let you know I am well.
I know you have your lives to live, and your interests, but I
have only myself, and this life of which you know nothing.
I do try to make my letters as meaningful as possible.

My friends here can't even communicate with me, but
show me by actions that they love me and want my love

and kindness, so I can live in a sort of feeling wanted and needed existence.

When Raja and I finish the eye examinations, I will have had a personal contact with everyone here. Of them, there are hundreds who have never before had any contact with an educated or a kind, understanding soul.

Living with anyone, day in and day out, is so difficult, and I know Mabel feels the same about me. I think, sometimes, there must be something good and fine about her, if I can only find it. I am trying to love her.

November 20, 1967

Mr. Bhatia asked for the addresses of all my children. I thought he might fear I'd wither away, but instead he wanted to write to my sons—he was embarrassed that I even thought he meant to include my daughters. He would NEVER write to a strange woman!

I am beginning to think of Christmas, and what all of you are doing, getting ready for the holidays, and all the grandchildren being sweet for Santa Claus. I don't think I could stand it here, as I won't be able even to buy candy for all the little children, so I'm relieved that the Peace Corps is having all of us come to Goa to celebrate together.

There's a little excitement—we heard that there might be a drink available at Goa. I can't even imagine what a drink would be like after all this time!

November 26, 1967

An exciting package just got tossed over my transom. (That's how the postman delivers our mail.) I opened it, and there was my darling Mickey Spillane looking at me from the back of his book. Everything else was marked "Do not open until Christmas," and all I can say is, it's done up too darn good—won't even shake! But I will wait, not patiently, and I already love whatever it is.

Excuse me while I have a fit! I just had to open one package, and it was a can of TURNIP GREENS! I was starving, but I just didn't know what I was so hungry for— it was something green. I can hardly wait for dinnertime, this will be my very best meal in months.

November 30, 1967

How I wish you could see India through your own eyes. I know the sameness of my days must get boring, but I do have some experiences here that almost defy words.

I went to the Swami's place again last night. About 30,000 of us sat on the ground and listened avidly to him. Mr. Bhatia told me the Swami's life story. He was a bad boy until he was twenty-two, always in trouble, and one day he decided to change, so he went to a famous Swami in the Himalayas and asked to be taught. He was told he was no good, and was turned away. He persisted, and after living at college and studying philosophy for five years, he returned. He was turned away again, and was told that he must prove his sincerity by going without money all over India, earning his food day by day, and wearing only rags. After living like that for a year, he went back to the Swami, who observed him for a while, then told him to go out alone. He gave his first lecture in Bombay, and only twenty people attended, but after a month, a building wouldn't hold the crowds, so for years he has been lecturing outdoors.

Mr Bhatia wants me to be in the audience every night, but I am too old and decrepit to take that wild goose chase every night. Lordy, I have never been so hurried and pushed about—it's like trying to put Barnum and Bailey's Circus in my living room, if you can imagine 30,000 people trying to get on the same train at once.

December 2, 1967

I had a strange experience today. One of the patients is a tall young man who has TB. He went to Bombay today to have a lung operation. Before he left, he came by and asked me if I would pray to my god for him. Then he said he was also going to pray to his god, but he believed that mine might be a little kinder than his.

I am convinced that it was really intended for me to come to India. In fact, I believe it so strongly, I don't think I could have NOT come!

I broke my oath! I swore I wouldn't start another cross-word puzzle until I finished the one I started, but I haven't finished the first one yet, and had to move on. I didn't look up any answers in the back of the book, though. I work on them at the Clinic when I need a break, and it helps calm my temper.

That is one thing I have to watch—I blow up at the slightest provocation, and I did not, until recently. Something happens, my head gets tight, and I blow my top—then I get all right. Like, one day Aloo came by and said she had looked for me to go to lunch with her at the Central Office, and I said, "That's a big lie, you know where I was!" She admitted it, but I knew she just didn't have time to come looking for me, and I wouldn't have gone anyway, so her tale was unnecessary. But at least she doesn't know that it's an insult to be called a liar.

Oh, my good mood is back! We went to the German Consul General's home for dinner, and I ate roast beef and bread! It was quite an occasion, so I wore my green chiffon dress. I had washed it, and it shrank so, I didn't think I'd ever get into it again, but I dragged it out and pressed it—and it fit perfectly! All the Germans were so hospitable, and we were served drinks, so that made it a happy evening for all of us.

Some of the other PCV's were there, and I learned that we were thought by many Indians to be working with U.S. Intelligence. Good grief!

A lot of the PCV's wanted to know what kind of reducing diet I'd been on to lose so much weight, because they wanted to reduce. I just said, "Come eat with us, you'll lose." We have been unable to get bread since the bakery is closed, and we can't get eggs, butter or oil anymore, but the canned milk and grits from the food parcels have been lifesavers. I know, I know, when we are really hungry, we can eat stewed rat!

December 12, 1967

Night before last, I had just turned off my lights and gone to bed when this terrible noise started. I thought a huge plane was about to hit the house! As the noise became earsplitting, my fan stopped, my bed started shaking, and for a whole minute or more, my WHOLE LIFE was before me! Finally, everything became calm, and I could hear frightened voices outside. I ran to Mabel, because I couldn't stand being alone. Don't ever let anybody tell you that an earthquake won't scare the wits out of you!

All day yesterday, hundreds of workers stayed home because they were so frightened, and those of us who went to work as usual talked in whispers all day!

Now, I can just sit here and write while the tremors are going on. I think my ability to be frightened is gone forever—I will just continue whatever I'm doing, because I know that running or fear will not help at all when it's time for me to go . . .

December 19, 1967

You will never know the happiness I'm spreading with the perfumes and knives you sent months ago for me to share with my friends here. You'll also never know how much willpower it has taken to keep from keeping some of it for myself. I'm fixing up a little package for Mr. Vinod, who gave me a tiny pine tree. When I saw the little tree, I choked, but I will NOT give way to my feelings, and I'm going to put something on it for decoration, and put my gifts under it (I hid them in my suitcase to relieve my temptation), and I WILL celebrate Christmas! I will rush through it here, and put my homesickness aside. Then I'll be free to go to the Peace Corps celebration in Goa, and pretend I'm Santa, spreading joy and happiness for all the other PCV's who will be there, and who haven't had as many great holidays at home to remember as I have. I am going to surprise Mabel with a gift Christmas morning. That will make her mad, since she's not giving me anything, and there's no way for me to explain to her that the gift is for my happiness, not hers!

(ABOUT 275 MILES SOUTH OF BOMBAY)

December 25, 196/

What a wonderful day! All the others went out on the
town last night, and I stayed at the hotel to do my own
celebrating! As soon as everyone was out of sight, I went
down to the kitchen and just took over the supervision of
preparing the Christmas dinner. Everything turned out
perfectly, and the food looked like a picture. We had twelve
turkeys, stuffing, salad, and all the trimmings.

I had forgotten I could cook, but it kept me from thinking of all of you, and when the others actually applauded
when they saw the tables, it made my day complete—I
hope your Christmas was as happy as mine!

❧ 13/6 GODREJ COLONY—VIKHROLI

January 2, 1968

I loved all the gifts you all sent me for Christmas, and
I'm almost afraid to write this letter, but I hope you will
understand. On New Year's my friends here have a custom
of exchanging gifts as we do for Christmas. I realized that
their kindness to me was the one thing that sustains me—
and I gave all my gifts away, one by one. I couldn't help it.

I had already had the joy of receiving them, and I just had no other way to pass that joy along to these people who have come to mean so much to me.

I laugh when I realize how ridiculous my life must seem to all of you. Mabel had a fit over my gift to her, it was the only thing she wanted—a jar of mustard!

January 4, 1968

I have been invited to join a weekly Discussion Group. It is on Hindu religion and Mr. Bhatia invited me. He is the nicest person I have ever met. He is so shy, he clasps his hands in front of himself so he doesn't have to shake hands. I believe he would lay down his life for me, and I certainly don't want that. You have seen people who are so damned good you can't imagine that they go to the bathroom—well, that's how he is.

I expect they will want me to say something at the discussion—well, whatever I say, they'll never know the difference.

Religion, as such, means so little to me now, just people, and their problems—hunger, housing, clothes. Oh, God, I have seen it all. I can never again take bread or warmth for granted.

Never before have I felt such a need to feel close to my family. I look back through the letters from my children, my sisters, even my brothers, and I find that knowing someone cares is my only means of survival.

Around me are threats of war, an unsettled and confused country, ugly looks, not to mention the earthquakes. When things seem unbearable, I think of my family.

But, enough of that—a miracle happened today, and I had a moment of silent rejoicing. Dr. Bhatia said he had an "efficient nurse." So there are some events that will stand out in my future as pillars of fire.

Things seem to come to us so fast at times in our lives, we wonder if we will survive—but, somehow, we always do.

I think back to times when I was young, when I would have given up my life just to be rid of some worry, when I just knew the time would never come when I would be happy again. Suddenly, the sun would shine, the crisis had passed, and all would be all right again.

You are my children, and, as such, you have a tendency to overcome difficulties, so just remember me at certain times of your youth and say, "Mother did not go completely under, and I won't either!"

Sometimes, I think my coming to India was a completely

selfish move. I left all personal worries behind me, and am in another world, where my worries are not personal, but of such huge proportions that it takes more than just me to overcome them—so, "Come on, God, this is your problem!" And He answers.

January 15, 1968

When I was in Goa, I bought a beautiful cashmere shawl. The weather here is colder than ever in history, so I wore my shawl to the Clinic today. One of the patients came in with pneumonia, and since we have no blankets, I wrapped my shawl around him, and let him wear it on home. Material things have lost all meaning for me.

I still have insomnia, but instead of lying awake trying to rearrange the universe, I think only of home. But when I imagine arriving at the Atlanta Airport, a feeling of fear comes over me. I wonder why???

One of the Peace Corps workers told me that she served her commitment and when she returned to America, she went through such a "culture shock" it became unbearable, so she volunteered to come back to India. I've never heard of "culture shock," but I wonder if it won't be hard to be surrounded by so many white people, and I can't remember how that must be.

You see the kind of things I worry about—things nobody else ever even thinks of.

I go regularly to the Discussion Group now, and have even been taking part in the discussions. The others are all men, and I like that! Since we sit on the floor, I wear my slacks, and Mr. Bhatia approves. He is so nice, but objects to my riding with a Muslim or on a scooter, or even walking at night. I feel sure he must object to my short dresses, so wherever I go, I have a scarf to drape over my knees.

On the other hand, Dr. Bhatia likes for me to talk about American miniskirts. He has the idea that all American women have six husbands and are immoral—I think he envies them.

So you see, I do have a diversified life. I talk with some of the Swami's top followers as an equal, but I was invited to speak at a medical meeting about the difference in American and Indian medicines. I told them I was not permitted to speak on any subject about comparisons, because that could be construed as "political." I didn't give them the real reason—that I don't have enough sense!

January 21, 1968

Had a taste of "back home" fun at a picnic! What did I find? A friendly bunch playing their version of rummy for *money*. There were eight players, sitting on three beds pushed together. I just climbed up and joined them. They said they wanted some American money—famous last words! I won two out of every three games.

I took some pictures at the picnic, and will ask Mr. Bhatia to mail the film from Bombay. If you receive it, please have it developed and mail the prints to me. These people have never had a photo taken before, and most have never seen a color one.

Mr. Vinod asked to see the camera, and snapped a picture of me with his little girl.

January 26, 1968

The Group has been discussing the trend of young people following the Swami in the Himalayas. People here are disappointed at his publicity in America, and think that some are using him for a fad. All the Swamis that I have heard of are from the same group, or studied with him, or are his students.

Frankly, they all seem to be fabulously rich. "Our" Swami has a beautiful camp near here. Mr. Bhatia sits as a Swami does, and acts like one. Although I don't believe a word, I am interested, enjoy it a lot, and it's so different.

That reminds me of enjoyable, different pastimes I had at home. Some of the happiest times I had were going to the wrestling matches and eating hot dogs and having a screaming fit over the matches. I wonder who the champion is now.

February 1, 1968

This is funny weather. The wind blows cold and chaps my hands, while the sun burns at the same time. Most of the people here actually believe that unseasonable weather, particularly earthquakes, is caused by Americans exploding bombs, and the vibrations are coming through the earth and upsetting the other side. It really is COLD early in the mornings, and everyone goes about shaking. I get right sick to my stomach when I see the little shivering, naked children coming to the Clinic to be treated for pneumonia. I gave that pretty striped sweater to the sweeper—he thought it was the prettiest thing he'd ever seen. It probably had a moth hole in it anyhow.

February 6, 1968

My work is the same all the time, so I seldom mention it anymore. One of the men came to the Clinic today and told me he was leaving for Malaysia, and I just started crying. How on earth will I feel when the time comes for me to leave, and I have to tell my people good-bye forever?

Dr. Bhatia has a fit when anyone comes to see me because he thinks everyone tries to take advantage of me, and he sticks to the idea that it should be everyone for himself. Today he brought me a picture of himself, and I was really touched, for he does not have a single speck of sentiment in him. He is huffy now because my radio is visiting the telephone operator for a week. He stays in the office alone at night and the watchman comes in between rounds to listen with him.

February 9, 1968

Sunday, Mabel and Aloo went off without me, since I had made my plans to wash my clothes, curl up in a chair, and have a really big cry!

My doorbell rang, and I answered it (in housecoat and barefoot). It was a friend of Jimmy's, Mr. Fendler, who was in Bombay on business. He insisted I get dressed and go to the Taj Hotel in Bombay with him for dinner. So, instead of a bawl, I had a ball!

He was a big talker, and I just loved him. We ate with some of his friends, and I blush with shame at some of the things he said about me—about my wealth, background, and so on—but, honestly, I needed it for my morale.

We had a gorgeous looking steak dinner, but I could not eat it, not even half of it—I have probably lost my taste for good food.

I bought a new book, "Jane Austen's Complete Works in One Volume." I really believe this one will last me until I come home! You know her! No man ever touched the HEM of a lady's garment, didn't even call their wives by first names—I could never understand where their children came from.

Which reminds me, we don't advocate the loop anymore—pills, vasectomies and tubectomies only, and one in a thousand women have intellect enough to take pills. One lady told me she solved "not forgetting" by taking seven on Monday for the whole week.

I'm talking about everything else, to keep from telling you that I stayed home from work yesterday for the first time since I've been here. I was just simply exhausted, and was too tired to sleep.

Well, that's enough grunting. I'm O.K. now, and worked all day today.

Exciting news! Our Swami is going to lecture at Kendra, and I have been invited to meet him. Mr. Bhatia is one of the chief students, and he said I will be introduced to the Swami by him alone. That is indeed a high honor. I can hardly wait! I have even been informed that I will be permitted to kiss AT his feet, if I so desire!

Raja is wonderful to me. He walked with me to the village today, through masses of people, lepers, beggars, cows, goats—but we made it. I cannot walk in the village alone, because people throng around me so I can't get through.

Oh, if I had words to describe this life and my constant longing to change just one hopeless life into something pertaining to HOPE or LOVE or even CHARITY—but charity is something they do not want, or even understand.

Even Mr. Vinod, who brightens my world with his beautiful flowers, and gives me the only vegetables I have, will not accept a gift from me in return. I have a beautiful hand-carved Krishna, and he thinks it is wonderful. It is his, of course, but I cannot give it to him until I leave because he would consider it too valuable to be acceptable.

February 22, 1968

Happy Birthday, George Washington! Sorry, Mr. President, but we don't know you here, so instead we. will be celebrating the anniversary of "To Whom It May Concern" next Monday.

Yesterday our neighbor had a foreign visitor, and they wanted to borrow a roll of toilet paper for the occasion, which was quite unusual. In each bathroom there is a cup and a tap—they pour a little water in their hands, and rinse off after doing their business—that is the reason they never eat with their left hands. (I made Raja explain to me in detail. It is a delicate subject, and one I couldn't discuss with just anybody.)

February 24, 1968

Happy news from home! Billy and Sybil's little Mandy has arrived. She and Amy will be a joy for me when I get home. I think of all my children and grandchildren; and cannot bear to linger over my thoughts. The sun is shining, and it would be heaven to be at my pond now, fishing. (Also, I'd have a big, cold chocolate milkshake!)

I just looked at the pictures stuck in my mirror, and it dawned on me I haven't seen the back of my head since I've been here—if I did, I might kill myself. When Raja thinks it looks too bad, he takes the scissors and does something to the back, and I still cut whatever sticks out in front.

February 25, 1968

No wonder I get so exhausted—mentally and physically! Mentally, because it takes all my senses to engage in conversation for hours at a time without answering political questions or being critical of things that are so different.

Physically, well, if you can visualize my sitting on a rug chanting to Krishna (or somebody) for five minutes to get in a spiritual mood before our teacher goes into his lecture, and then sitting cross-legged for an hour listening, then stumbling home with two or three escorts who would not catch me if I were falling (because they are too pure to touch any woman other than their wives), then dragging myself up three flights of stairs, after having been on my feet since daybreak—then you truly have a photographic mind!

I'm going out now to walk up the mountain and sit and read, where I can be quiet and alone. I have to hide behind a rock, or I will be surrounded by natives who come from nowhere and squat and stare and giggle.

February 28, 1968

I thought the time would never come, but I finally met the great Swami Chinmayananda. He spoke, then answered questions, and that was terrific—but afterwards, our Discussion Group met him personally, and I was allowed to take two photos of him, and even got to chat with him for a few minutes. The greatest part of all, though, was the fact that he LOOKED at me once—this is considered the highest honor of all!

Every day here is getting to be more valuable than the last. I feel a need to keep every little happening in my mind.

I cannot stand to think of anything bad happening to my children or my grandchildren while I'm gone. I have no stamina—I just have people fooled. ENOUGH!

Did I tell you the good news? Mr. Bhatia told me that he will shake my hand the day I leave India.

I have been thinking about the Swami's lecture, and he said one thing I will never forget, "If you are good, be DYNAMICALLY good, don't be passively anything!"

He went on to explain that regardless of any criticism, do what you think is right.

Someone asked him about comparing Jesus with any other great man, and he gave as an example that Hitler sacrificed the world to save himself, but Jesus sacrificed Himself to save the world.

I have nearly all his books, and I hope someday I'll have another chance to hear him—or see him, which is just as good.

I have two new friends I'd like you to meet. One is Joglekar, who is a great lover of books, and the other is Jonny, who sells ivory carvings. Jonny came by here one evening to make a fortune off "The Rich American." I found that I HAVE learned to say "No!" He has really beautiful things, and God knows where he gets them. His prices are much cheaper than I've seen anywhere else, so I might just buy a few things and have them mailed to you.

Joglekar comes by occasionally, to talk about books, or to play bridge. He and I went to see a movie, "Hurry Sundown." Everyone wanted my reaction because it was about the "South"—but the best thing about the evening was that we had a nice dinner afterwards!

March 6, 1968

Well, I know one thing—since I've been wearing chappals, I'll never become accustomed to wearing shoes again! Please send me some pictures showing styles in America. I can't even imagine how tacky I would look in my outfits here, in comparison.

Everybody had a fit over the pictures you had developed for me. I have to keep my camera hidden now, because everyone wants to have a photo made.

I got some things from the salesman, Jonny. I found out where he gets them—he has a man who does all the carving, and when I ask him about something, he gets it done and brings it to me, so I can't refuse to buy some of it. He is mailing a package, so I hope it gets there!

March 10, 1968

This is all I know:

If Mr. Macini comes in, he gets an injection to help him combat fatigue.

Mr. Patil has a stomach ulcer and comes in for sympathy. He doesn't believe it's caused by what he eats, although I see his belly waddling in half a minute before I see his face.

Mr. Kantiwalla's moans reach my ears in time for me to get his injection ready and be waiting for him by the time he reaches my office.

I know who is pregnant, how many children everyone has, and whether they use contraceptives or not.

I'm BORED with all that, and the moral of this letter is:

I'm homesick, and getting more so every day.

I wish I could keep from counting the days until I come home in September—but I can't.

March 13, 1968

Our food is getting slim, but thanks to Mr. Vinod I'm cooking carrots and beets for supper. What I'm starving for is something to read!

When we don't have food, I try to think of pleasant things, like watching "Bonanza" and Dean Martin on TV. I wonder if I'll be afraid to be alone when I get home—I know I've changed, but I can't explain it. I'm not afraid of anything here—I trust everyone. What would I be afraid of at home—white people?

These people believe in horoscopes, and theirs are different from the books we see at home. They even have their wives and husbands selected by their horoscopes. I don't pay a bit of attention to stuff like that, but today mine said not to travel—and I'm not.

March 15, 1968

Last night Mr. and Mrs. Joglekar came over to play bridge. Later we went out on my balcony and sat in the cool breeze. Oh, it was so beautiful! There was a full moon, and stars. On the hillside were the little lights twinkling in the huts, and in the distance, the Bay with small boat lights. Sometimes, I forget to look at beauty.

Right now, I am enjoying the lovely things on my writing table. I have a rosewood box, the carved Krishna, salt and pepper shakers, a little ivory Gandhi, a fly swatter, some pigeon mess and a sponge.

Jonny came by to see me, and brought me a little bottle of brandy. I took a swig tonight, but, frankly, it didn't cheer me up. Goodnight . . . as I look out my window, I see the moon, and I know that somewhere, someone is thinking of me, and that God is looking at me, so I am not quite alone.

March 17, 1968

In the paper today, I read that Bobby Kennedy would announce his decision to run for President. All Indians seem to welcome the news, and I'm anxious to hear the reaction there, especially in my family. God knows what will happen, but at least we have news from America in the paper here now. I have decided I'm for RFK, because I've always loved him, and saw the picture of him and Ethel with the children, which shows he's a good Catholic. At any rate, I have something to look forward to in the paper each day, and I'm so excited—I feel so much closer to home!

March 20, 1968

Oh, I'm so glad you got the package. You loved the Madonna? Good grief, I thought it was just a carving of a naked lady! And, yes, that IS a chess set, and it's for Billy! The ice-cream spoons are for Amy. I'll get something for everyone else to bring home when I come. Jonny has finally realized that his "rich American" customer is poorer than he is, so now he just drops in for a chat when he's in the neighborhood.

I've been reading my horoscope every day, simply because Dr. Bhatia enjoys my acting stupid enough to show an interest in it. He only considers food and work important, so I am the most frivolous person he's ever met, and I love to shock him. He said the other day that when I first came he couldn't follow my words at all, and couldn't understand anything in an American movie, but that now he can understand everything I say, and he saw a Dean Martin movie lately, and understood every word. Actually, he doesn't have the foggiest notion what I'm talking about half the time—but he tries.

March 25, 1968

I had to tear up the letter I wrote yesterday, because I was just too sad to be unemotional, and I hurt so much, I started to cry—and I don't allow myself that luxury. I had a letter from the Peace Corps saying they had planned to let us out early, but they had to rescind the order, so now we will be here until the middle of September. Today I am saying, "What the Hell, so I have to stay away from home five weeks longer than I thought—so what?" Even though it seems like an eternity to me, I will have to stand it, so I will not gripe.

One thing about it, I am pleased that Dr. Bhatia is happy over it.

Please be a little disappointed for my sake, and when I do come home, don't let me ever go away again.

Jonny is going to bring me a package of Pall Malls. Since we have become buddies, he has admitted he can get anything for a price. He also confessed that at first he thought I was a spy.

Little Gandhi just sits here on my table, reading his Bible —he never looks up.

I am tired, and tense. I am going to take my vacation in Madras. Joglekar brought me ten magazines to take with me, so I will have something to read.

Every day in the papers, I read more and more about Bobby Kennedy, and it seems that Johnson is not going to run. It is so exciting to have political news from America, and I feel almost a part of the campaigns. Surely, there's no one in the world who's more interested than I!

Thank God for vacation time! I need rest so badly.

ᕫᔓ M A D R A S

April 1, 1968

Did I say vacation?

I have been here just long enough to find Prohibition, they speak Tamil, it's hotter than Vikhroli, and I'm sick! I don't know what's wrong with me, but my stomach is so sore I can't bend, and I have terrific pains in my back.

All the things I have to read, I'm sure I've read in a previous life (when I was back in the U.S.). However, until I feel better, I am just going to lie here and read and rest. Actually, it's lovely to be a little indisposed with a stack of magazines, and I'm sure the pain will go away in a little while.

✑ 13/6 GODREJ COLONY—VIKHROLI

April 14, 1968

I came home two days ago. I just had to be near someone I know. The "little pain" turned out to be an attack of renal colic—and I hope I never hear of it again!

I flew back to Bombay and got a taxi to bring me home. So far, I haven't been able to do anything, I've been so sore, but I'm going to work tomorrow and work as long as I feel like it. I will have to forget my pain and not anticipate another attack.

I'm feeling better already, so by the time you get this you'll know I'm well!

We are all so upset over Martin Luther King's death, and I have just had to answer queries by comparing it to Gandhi's assassination. I cannot explain it, but when I read of the death of any American, my heart breaks, and I grieve as though it is a personal loss. Somehow, I am attuned to sadness, and all Americans seem like part of my family.

When I read about it, I was glad that Mrs. King had such a nice escort, and how I would love to hear Belafonte sing right now. He's always been my special favorite.

I wonder how I can live so closely to black people, love them, and ever be able to return to Plains and feel any differently.

It's so hot and humid today! Come to think of it, what the hell is "humid," anyway? I just know it would be a pleasure to faint, but I was too busy.

Our icebox has been out for a week—nothing but warm water to drink, and no place for eggs and stuff. Mabel and I are planning a big celebration (Jello!) when it gets fixed. It really does one good to HAVE to do without—to make us appreciate more!

I missed getting my last food parcel, but now I don't panic, because if I don't get all of them, maybe someone hungrier does.

April 25, 1968

I am sitting at a Medical Association meeting, pretending I'm taking notes while I write this. They had a seat for me in the front row, but my dress was too short, so I'm in the second row, surrounded by men—there's not another woman in the house!

I brought my camera so I could take a picture of the FOOD at the luncheon. I came with Dr. Bhatia, who yelled at another driver, "He know not he go the Hell!" I love to go places with him because I always am so relaxed around him, and he likes having me.

I don't lack for a topic of conversation today, because they all want to discuss Martin Luther King and the Presidential election.

Here's the guest speaker—he has a soprano voice. I'll stop until after lunch and tell you all we have to eat.

Shucks! All Indian food! I ate, though!

~§ 13/6 GODREJ COLONY—VIKHROLI

April 28, 1968

I'm so homesick! I'm sitting here looking at pictures of all of you on the mirror in front of me. Everyone is smiling at me, and I'm trying so hard to smile back!

I guess you wonder how I can write so many letters—well, I have no TV, no company, no reading material, no car—and I couldn't stand to just sit and look at Mabel. If you take all these things out of your life, you'll find plenty of writing time. (Figure that out.)

Since Rockefeller announced, the Presidential race is even more exciting. You have so many things to think of you can afford not to get excited over politics, but I know, deep down, you are interested, because the clippings you send arc terrific!

I'm trying to be real sweet to Mabel, because I'm looking forward to her going on vacation with such great delight. Even Aloo and Joglekar are going, but I'll be left with the dear old Clinic, plenty of work, and Raja to go shopping with me, so I'll have a great time!

May 5, 1968

Mr. Bhatia and his family came to call on me. I had no idea what to serve, but decided on Mangola (a cold soft drink) and some sort of cookies. I fixed a peanut butter and jelly sandwich for their little girl, and presented them with a carved Krishna as a "Thank you" for my visit in their home. His friendship and words of wisdom have been such an important part of my life these past few months.

I really don't know how I survive. If I live to be a hundred, I'll never begin to tell you everything that has happened to me—never. But I won't live that long. Do you know, I only have a few more years to live? THAT'S a dull thought! The life expectancy here is forty-seven, and I'm nearly seventy, so I think I'm lucky!

May 8, 1968

I have tried and tried to think, but I cannot remember. Will you please describe cold weather for me? When Mabel's vacation ends, we'll have one more monsoon, and then I'll be coming home. That's how I keep track of time here. I've got to get my mind ready to return to America, so I won't feel this panic at the difference!

Our Peace Corps Director came to see me from Bombay. He brought me a bottle of Scotch, which, he said, was very good for renal colic. He also said he had a letter from Senator Humphrey about me. I don't know what was in the letter, but the Director is sending a car for me one day next week so I can go to the office and have assistance getting my termination papers filled out, AND I'LL HAVE A STEAK DINNER!

When he left, he turned around and asked, "Who the Hell ARE you, Lilly?"

May 12, 1968

I'm low. I won't dare eat any of Mabel's food while she's away, and it's been over two months since I had a food parcel. It is not the season for vegetables, but Mr. Vinod sends me lovely flowers even more often when food is scarce. He just sent some stuff like we have at home (yellow) that makes hay fever. Can't think of the name of it.

Did I tell you he showed me how to keep flowers fresh? Fill a bucket half full of water, dip the heads of the flowers in it, then cover all of the stems in the bucket overnight. They keep for days then.

I'm looking out at my mountain and the lights. It's so peaceful. What do you call that yellow stuff?

You know, I just realized how full of ME my letters are —please forgive me—I have hundreds of others to write about, but you don't know or have any idea of them, so what can I write of but me?

May 15, 1968

I had so much mail yesterday, the postman brought it to the Clinic. He was as happy as I was, and all the patients were breathing down my neck, looking over my shoulder and opening everything—none of which they could make heads or tails of. There were some pictures of Billy's children, and everybody just loved them, but could not understand the blond hair! It was bedlam, and I'm glad Dr. Bhatia wasn't there. He's on leave because his brother is getting married.

There are two young doctors, taking his place, and we get along fine. When they order something we don't have, they say, "Just substitute." They give my patients a lot of attention, and I just love that!

That yellow stuff is driving me nuts. Hurry and tell me what it is!

May 20, 1968

The trip to the P.C. office was enjoyable, but if I could have found the energy to think of a good reason to go home early (and if the Peace Corps would pay my way) I would have given it. I had planned to do some shopping while I was in Bombay, but I couldn't think of a thing I want.

I already have a real luxury—a can of fly killer and a sprayer. I'm enjoying it to the utmost!

I am waiting for my friend Joglekar to come by. He gave me a copy of "Wuthering Heights," which I have finished reading for the tenth time. I'm looking at the fresh flowers that Mr. Vinod sent . . .

It's Goldenrod!!!

Well, Dr. Bhatia's brother got married, and I went on a chartered bus with about two hundred relatives. It was fantastic to watch dear Dr. Bhatia in the midst of it all. I won't go into details, but, one thing, the bride and her folks came in a taxi, and after the taxi drove away, they discovered that they had left the groom's clothes, the bride's saris, and the 10,000 rupee dowry in the taxi! Much dispute came up, and for a while we thought they'd have to take the bride back, but she finally came on home with the groom, and they're honeymooning at Dr. Bhatia's flat—three rooms, and twenty-five guests sleeping there!

The food package arrived. Now maybe I won't be so completely exhausted. I never realize I've been hungry until I get something to eat.

I have the house all shining and ready for Mabel's return. I'm as glad to see her come home as I am to see her go.

I touched home!

A busload of Americans came through, and I rushed out to exchange greetings with them. I said I was from Georgia, and a young man said, "Hey, I'm from Georgia," and stuck his head out the window. He said, "Where are you from?" and I said, "Plains." Then he said, "Are you Mrs. Carter?"

Somebody remembered me! He said, "I'm from Koinonia Farms." Oh, right down the road from home—I wanted to grab him, I was so GLAD to see someone from HOME.

But the bus had to drive on.

June 7, 1968

I just can't take it.

I just can't take any more so far from home!

Everyone rushed to me for consolation when we got the news of Bobby Kennedy's death, but I had none to give.

My heart is broken.

June 9, 1968

I am miserable, and I hate Sundays!

It is afternoon, and I still have on my nightgown, and I just don't care.

I don't care who gets the nomination now—I just want tomorrow to come, and I want to come home!

June 16, 1968

I feel better now, and turned on Voice of America tonight, but they had a symphony orchestra playing, so I
turned it off again. Some things are worse than nothing.

Joglekar came by and brought me a "new" book he
thought maybe I hadn't read—"Huckleberry Finn." I hope
I can read it, though it's a little sophisticated for me!

My clothes are all threadbare, because I have to wash
them so often. I don't want any more, though, and I'll just
leave everything here when I leave anyway.

June 20, 1968

You couldn't imagine that some of these people do nothing manual. The cashier at the bank has a servant to pick
up the phone and hand it to him when it rings. Then when
he finishes the conversation, he rings a bell and the servant
rushes back to replace the receiver. Now, the phone is
within two feet of the cashier!

They laugh at me for being considerate of servants, and
when I tell them I wash my dishes and do my own cooking,
they don't believe me.

I wipe off the injection table and chairs at the Clinic, and
anyone else would lose face by doing that. I love to shock
them, and they bring their friends to watch me wash off a
cabinet!

When I bandage a foot or leg, my patient bends down, puts a hand on each of my feet, and salaams.

I am Memsahib, and Madame, and Monshey, and Sister, and one calls me Little Mama. I can understand their native tongues, and talk with basic words and gestures—and I love them, and they love me.

June 25, 1968

Push, push, push—I am trying to skoot the time away. I hope it will slow down when I get home, so I can sit in the sun and fish!

You know I never think when I fish, and Boy! Does my brain need a vacation! I don't care whether I catch anything or not—I will have so many things to forget, and many to remember always.

Every day, my mind is strained to its limit. As always, I try too hard to be efficient, and at my age, it's difficult.

I gave Joglekar my "Gone With the Wind." I had to give him something in return for the books he gave me—and I did read "Huckleberry Finn" (for the hundredth time)—and, what is more, I did enjoy it!

I'm rich, rich, rich! I have two bars of Lux soap! I went on a shopping spree, and paid five rupees a bar!

July 1, 1968

I have just worried God to death to please let my food parcel come before I gave out—and today it came! I cannot put anything up for a rainy day, because the monsoon is already here.

We haven't really had a water shortage here, but in a lot of places they don't even have drinking water. The hill folks have to carry water a mile up the hill—some have never had a complete bath (not that they want one).

I don't think anyone here has ever heard of a tranquilizer, and anyway, they don't believe in them. I thought of it because I can't sleep if I have the smallest worry. I lie awake for hours, and talk to myself to get over it.

I'm going to the Swami's camp with Mr. Bhatia—he goes to rest and meditate. I'm invited to stay for a few days and commute to work, but Dr. Bhatia wouldn't allow me to do that, he said I would get too tired.

July 6, 1968

The Swami's camp was so peaceful, and I did stay overnight. Mr. Bhatia is the teacher, since the Swami isn't there. At any rate, it was something different, and I loved it.

Jonny mailed a few things for me—I've decided he must be honest. Anyway, he brings a little sunshine into our lives, and takes a few rupees out as he leaves.

149

I'm trying to remember what a day in my life was like in America. I imagine going to church on Sunday, going out for lunch, fishing in my pond, having a cold toddy, running by to see what you were watching on TV, grandchillun running in and out of the house—Boy, I didn't know how lucky I was!

I have forgotten any pleasure, except doing for these poor people, and I can't brag on myself, because that's all I have to do.

July 14, 1968

I love the constant rain. I know I won't have to go anywhere except to work, and even when the sun comes out, I'm too tired to go up on the roof. In less than two months I will be leaving, and Dr. Bhatia worries about my going; it's probably because I am free labor, but actually he has forgotten what the others did before I came.

My days are all the same now—smiling, working and passing the hours as best I can. I can't get anything on VOA because of so much static, but hear plenty about Congress wanting to cut Foreign Aid. I just tell everybody who asks to wait till I get back to America, and I will straighten it out. I wish all the aid would go straight to Dr. Bhatia to let him help my patients, and then I would know that the really poor are getting it.

I am getting upset, and I don't want to think before I go to bed, so I will stop . . .

July 20, 1968

Though I try to write, I feel sometimes that my letters seem so morbid. I have a lot to do before I leave, and even have to go to Bombay to go through final termination—I don't know why—all I want is to get on a plane and go to Georgia!

I had a letter from some friends in Florida, wanting me to come down after I get home, and talk about my life in India. That scares the hell out of me. I would worry more about making a speech than anything else—just thinking about it gives me nervous prostration! Maybe later on I will think of something funny to say, but I can think of nothing humorous as of now.

Maybe, someday, I'll even be able to laugh about these ragged clothes I'm wearing—but now all I think of them is that you might be ashamed of me.

July 26, 1968

I don't have enough rupees to write often, so when you get a letter, please call the others and let them know that I'm all right.

I'm getting nervous about coming home—you know, like worms crawling under my skin. But everyone is so sweet to me at the Clinic—they act like I'm going to die. I am such a fool, but I have tears that pop up every time anyone talks about my leaving. They hate to see me go, and I don't understand why I should feel tearful, for God knows I am dying to get home!

August 4, 1968

I went into Bombay for the "termination" conference. All the PCV's who came when I did (rather those of us who haven't quit or been sent home for medical reasons) were there. I doubt that we will ever hear of each other again in the U.S.A.

Gosh, how the time is flying! The closer the time comes, the more upset I get about coming home. Why? I don't know, but I am . . .

And yet, it keeps me so excited to think I am so near, and yet so far.

August 9, 1968

I spend my spare time packing, and then I take out all the things I want to leave, so now, the only thing I have left to bring is my radio. I would never part with that. Do they still have radios there? It is such a treasure here, and I cannot imagine that I could ever replace it.

My friends here have started giving me little presents, so I will have those precious gifts to pack.

I am being entertained royally, and accept every invitation —teas, luncheons, dinners—and, best of all, bridge with the Joglekars. Am feeling grand and excited, but have a feeling of great sadness when anyone says good-bye.

August 15, 1968

I am seventy years old today, and I think of where I am, and what I'm doing, and why.

When Earl died, my life lost its meaning and direction. For the first time, I lost my will to live. Since that time, I've tried to make my life have some significance. I felt useful when I was at Auburn, serving as housemother for my bad, sweet K.A.'s. And I'm glad I worked at the Nursing Home, but God forbid that I ever have to live in one!

I didn't dream that in this remote corner of the world, so far away from the people and material things that I had always considered so necessary, I would discover what Life is really all about. Sharing yourself with others, and accepting their love for you, is the most precious gift of all.

If I had one wish for my children, it would be that each of you would dare to do the things and reach for goals in your own lives that have meaning for you as individuals, doing as much as you can for everybody, but not worrying if you don't please everyone.

When I look back over my life, I see the pieces fit—it has been a planned life, and I truly believe God had everything to do with it.

August 20, 1968

I caused a small riot at Kendra today. Dr. Bhatia's sister gave me a sari blouse she'd made for me, and I put on my sari, and walked down to Kendra. Everyone just had a fit when I walked in. I've promised to wear it to our farewell function. They have a big party planned. Mabel and I will be guests of honor, and Dr. Bhatia will be the speaker (so the speech won't be more than two sentences).

I am excited, and terrified. I am so anxious to come home, but I feel so strange. As hard as I try, I cannot imagine how my life was back in America. Do the children remember me? I have nightmares that I will get off the plane and be surrounded by strange white people. I cannot fear the future, because it has no meaning for me. I wonder if I will be content to sit at home and read. Yes, I have had enough adventure to last me a lifetime.

This will be the last letter, because I will arrive in Atlanta Monday evening at 9:30. Please be at the airport by six, and wait for me—don't dare leave until I get there.

I saved my best dress to wear home. I know it will be falling apart by the time I get there, so please don't make fun of me.

All my friends are going to the airport in Bombay to say good-bye. How can I stand it, when I bawl at the very thought of leaving them—these wonderful people, for whom I've done so little, but who have done so much for me!

But, I do have one consolation—I'm coming home. Thank God.

I'M COMING HOME!